From despair

Insights into the book of Job

Peter Williams

DayOne

© Day One Publications 2002
First printed 2002

Scripture quotations are from The New King James Version.
© 1982 Thomas Nelson Inc.

British Library Cataloguing in Publication Data available
ISBN 1 903087 29 5

Published by Day One Publications
3 Epsom Business Park, Kiln Lane, Epsom, Surrey KT17 1JF.
☎ 01372 728 300 **FAX** 01372 722 400
email—sales@dayone.co.uk
www.dayone.co.uk

All rights reserved

No part of this publication may be reproduced, or stored in a retrieval system, or transmitted, in any form or by any means, mechanical, electronic, photocopying, recording or otherwise, without the prior permission of **Day One Publications.**

Designed by Steve Devane and printed by Creative Print and Design

Dedication
To the members and friends of
Moordown Baptist Church
who listened so patiently as I preached
through the book of Job

Author's Preface

I wish to make it clear at the outset that this is not, in any sense, a technical commentary dealing with the many critical questions associated with the book of Job, but is an exposition based on a series of Sunday morning sermons preached at Moordown Baptist Church, Bournemouth, from January 1989 to August 1990. I owe a debt of gratitude, therefore, to the members and friends of Moordown for their patience and faithfulness in allowing me to expound this profound book over such an extended period.

Job is undoubtedly one of the great books of the Bible, and one of the great treasures of the world's literature. In its literary structure it is a mixture of prose and poetry, the prologue and epilogue being narrative prose, and the main body of the book poetry. In my attempt to preach through Job, and then to write about it, I may well have bitten off more than I could chew, but that will be for you, the reader, to decide. My intention has been to explore the basic themes of undeserved suffering, the justice of divine government, the activities of Satan and the power of evil, the doctrines of double retribution and exact retribution, the meaning of wisdom and several others. My aim throughout has been directed to the ordinary reader by drawing from these themes lessons which are practical and relate to contemporary life.

I would like to express my deep appreciation to Dr JA Motyer for reading the manuscript and for his many valuable comments and helpful suggestions. Special thanks also to my dear friends Ruth and Brian Kerry for the expenditure of time and effort in typing and preparing the manuscript for publication.

Peter Williams
Bournemouth, 2002

Contents

- 1 JOB'S CHARACTER AND BACKGROUND — 9
- 2 GOD'S DIALOGUE WITH SATAN — 14
- 3 THE TESTING OF JOB — 20
- 4 JOB'S LAMENT — 26
- 5 YESTERDAY'S TESTIMONY, TODAY'S BLESSING — 31
- 6 SELF-JUSTIFICATION AND SELF-PITY — 39
- 7 BILDAD, AN UNSYMPATHETIC FRIEND — 45
- 8 MAN'S NEED OF RIGHTEOUSNESS — 50
- 9 GODLINESS WITHOUT WINSOMENESS — 57
- 10 HUMAN ARROGANCE — 62
- 11 TALKING THINGS THROUGH WITH GOD — 68
- 12 THE BREVITY OF LIFE — 74
- 13 WHAT IS MAN? — 80
- 14 MISERABLE COMFORTERS — 86
- 15 THE DOOM OF THE WICKED — 93
- 16 THE TRIUMPH OF FAITH — 98
- 17 WHY DO THE WICKED PROSPER? — 104
- 18 A BLEAK VIEW OF GOD — 109
- 19 THE GOD WHO HIDES — 115
- 20 GOD'S GREATNESS, MAN'S LITTLENESS — 120
- 21 JOB'S INTEGRITY — 126
- 22 THE NATURE OF WISDOM — 131

Contents

23 JOB'S GOLDEN PAST **136**

24 JOB'S PRESENT MISERY **142**

25 JOB'S TESTIMONY OF INNOCENCE **147**

26 A YOUNG MAN SPEAKS **156**

27 GOD'S SPOKESMAN **162**

28 THE JUSTICE OF GOD **171**

29 DOES IT PAY TO SERVE GOD? **180**

30 GOD, MAN AND NATURE **187**

31 GOD'S CHALLENGE TO JOB **198**

32 EPILOGUE **207**

6 From despair to hope

Plan of the Book of Job

Prologue (chapters 1 and 2)
    (a) Job's background (chapter 1:1–5)
    (b) The first test (chapter 1:6–22)
    (c) The second test (chapter 2:1–10)
    (d) Job's comforters (chapter 2:11–13)

Dialogue (chapters 3–27)
    Job's complaint (chapter 3:1–26)
First cycle of speeches (chapters 4–14)
    (a) Eliphaz's speech (chapters 4–5)
    (b) Job's response (chapters 6–7)
    (c) Bildad's speech (chapter 8)
    (d) Job's response (chapters 9–10)
    (e) Zophar's speech (chapter 11)
    (f) Job's response (chapters 12–14)
Second cycle of speeches (chapters 15–21)
    (a) Eliphaz's speech (chapter 15)
    (b) Job's response (chapters 16–17)
    (c) Bildad's speech (chapter 18)
    (d) Job's response (chapter 19)
    (e) Zophar's speech (chapter 20)
    (f) Job's response (chapter 21)
Third cycle of speeches (chapters 22–27)
    (a) Eliphaz's speech (chapter 22)
    (b) Job's response (chapters 23–24)
    (c) Bildad's speech (chapter 25)
    (d) Job's response (chapters 26–27)
Hymn of Wisdom (chapter 28)

Monologues (chapters 29:1–42:6)
Job: (a) His golden past (chapter 29)
    (b) His present misery (chapter 30)
    (c) His testimony of innocence
    (chapter 31)
Elihu: (a) His first speech (chapters 32–33)
    (b) His second speech (chapter 34)
    (c) His third speech (chapter 35)
    (d) His fourth speech (chapters 36–37)

God speaks (chapters 38:1–42:6)
    (a) The challenge to Job
    (chapters 38:1–40:2)
    (b) Job's response (chapter 40:3–5)
    (c) God speaks again
    (chapters 40:6–41:34)
    (d) Job's response (chapter 42:1–6)

Epilogue (chapter 42:7–17)
    (a) Verdict of the friends
    (chapter 42:7–9)
    (b) Job's restoration (chapter 42:10–17)

8 From despair to hope

Chapter 1

Job's character and background

Read Job 1:1–5

Who was Job, and what kind of man was he? Like the book named after him, he remains something of a mystery. We are told in the opening verse that he lived in the land of Uz, but this is not a great help since the actual location of Uz is uncertain. Some say it was situated in ancient Edom, while others place it somewhere in northern Arabia. Another intriguing question concerns the historicity of Job himself. Did he really exist? Some regard the book as a fictional work, a kind of parable intended to teach certain spiritual and moral truths. Others think it does not really matter whether Job actually lived or not, since the lessons taught in the book are still real and meaningful.

But I think it does matter. After all, the main theme of the book is the way in which Job succeeded in facing the most dreadful suffering without losing his faith in the love and justice of God. If, however, the account is fictitious, then it is small comfort to me, when faced with my own trials, to be told that Job did not actually exist and the book's teaching has no basis in real life. The truth is, however, that Job was a real person and he really did suffer the physical, spiritual and emotional anguish the book speaks about. In Ezekiel 14:14 he is commended for his proverbial righteousness alongside the historical figures of Noah and Daniel. James likewise (James 5:11) refers to Job as an example of perseverance in the face of trial and of what God accomplished in him and for him. He would hardly have used such an example if Job had been an imaginary character.

A godly man

So what kind of man was Job? His character is clearly delineated in the opening verse. 'This man was blameless and upright; he feared God and shunned evil.' This was God's own estimate of Job in the dialogue he

Chapter 1

initiates with Satan, leading to the assault upon Job's character. 'Then the Lord said to Satan, "Have you considered my servant Job? There is no one on earth like him; he is blameless and upright, a man who fears God and shuns evil"' (Job 1:8). He was a man of outstanding moral integrity on the *inside* of his life, with nothing crooked or deceitful about him; further, the words 'shunned evil' indicate that his life and behaviour *outwardly* was consistent with the state of his heart. He was the kind of man that others looked up to and had respect for in society. Later, when meditating on his past life, he recalls the esteem with which he was held in the community: 'When I went to the gate of the city and took my seat in the public square, the young men saw me and stepped aside and the old men rose to their feet' (Job 29:7–8). As a city counsellor his civic leadership was appreciated and his approval sought. But, for all that, we must not run away with the idea that the description 'blameless, upright … and shunned evil' meant that Job was sinless. Far from it.

Job himself was aware of that. In one of his darker moments of depression he cries out to God, 'Why do you not pardon my offences and forgive my sins?' (Job 7:21). He knew in the depths of his being that, in spite of his neighbours' high estimate of him, in the light of God's holiness he was a sinner. And any who, like Job, are morally upright and persons of integrity, but who think they are therefore not sinful, are deceiving themselves. As the apostle John says, 'If we claim to be without sin, we deceive ourselves and the truth is not in us' (1 John 1:8). Such a person is deluded and refuses to face up to the reality of the sinfulness of the human heart. For human nature is a paradox: on the one hand, a person is capable, like Job, of being morally upright and shunning what is evil; and yet on the other hand, under a different set of circumstances, that person is capable of the foulest acts of violence, lust and greed. We read of it every day in the newspapers and hear of it on the television. Man is an enigma to himself, therefore, and his nature confronts him with a problem he simply does not understand—the problem of sin.

The words 'blameless, upright … and shunned evil' *describe* Job's character, therefore, but do not *explain* it. That comes in the phrase 'a man who fears God'. That means he took God seriously, made him the centre of his life and worshipped him with reverence and godly fear. This was all the

Job's character and background

more remarkable, since he did not belong to Israel, the covenant people of God; he came from a pagan culture and background, like Abraham before him, but turned his heart toward God. Do we fear God? Do we take seriously the gospel of Jesus Christ in the midst of the pagan culture of our modern world? It is a great challenge, but it can be done. Job is proof of that, and that is why his experience is preserved in the revelation of Scripture. He is meant to be an encouragement to God's people, showing us that whilst our life can become at times a real battleground with the forces of evil, we can, with God's grace, overcome and gain the victory.

A wealthy man

Job was blessed with great material prosperity: 'he owned seven thousand sheep, three thousand camels, five hundred yoke of oxen and five hundred donkeys, and had a large number of servants. He was the greatest man among all the people of the East' (Job 1:3).

At this point in his life Job is not aware of any problem or tension arising out of the relationship between his faith in God on the one hand and his great material prosperity on the other. On the contrary, he lived at a time and in a culture when many believed that material wealth was a mark of divine blessing and a reward for godliness. But he was soon to suffer a rude awakening, when all his material possessions were suddenly taken from him and he was left entirely destitute. What now of God's favour and blessing, let alone his justice? This was an experience sufficient to shatter once for all Job's understanding of the loving character of God. But with the divine help he rose above it, as we shall see presently, and in spite of his perplexity his faith not only remained intact but was stronger at the end than at the beginning.

Wealth and spirituality are not necessarily incompatible, but it is hard to hold the tension between them, as is evident from our Lord's remark: 'How hard it is for the rich to enter the kingdom of God!' (Luke 18:24). It was because Job's fear of God and reverence for him were so deep and real that God was able to entrust him with great material possessions. That is not true of all believers. Some of us would not be able to handle great wealth in a way that would not affect our spiritual life and cause us to drift from the things of Christ. For although the Bible never condemns wealth itself, it

Chapter 1

nevertheless has plenty to say by way of warning to believers about the dangers associated with wealth and material possessions.

The truth is that a man's attitude to material things is one of the most exacting tests of a godly character. What a man does with material possessions, or what he allows material possessions to do to him, gives an illuminating insight into his true self. If we are not on our guard, money and material possessions can easily deaden the soul and take the edge off our spiritual life. What is more, we do not have to possess great wealth in order to love it and be possessed by it. That is the point Paul makes in his letter to Timothy: 'People who want to get rich fall into temptation and a trap and into many foolish and harmful desires that plunge men into ruin and destruction. For the love of money is a root of all kinds of evil. Some people, eager for money, have wandered from the faith and pierced themselves with many griefs' (1 Timothy 6:9–10). There are Christians who love money and whose lives are dominated by it even when they do not possess it. They are always thinking of it and longing to possess more of it, until this becomes their major preoccupation. It takes up their time and energy and fills their thoughts and inner life to such an extent that it becomes increasingly difficult for them to find time for God and the things of God. Pray that this may never happen to us.

The family man

The opening verses show Job as a happy man surrounded by a loving family. 'He had seven sons and three daughters … His sons used to take turns holding feasts in their homes, and they would invite their three sisters to eat and drink with them. When a period of feasting had run its course, Job would send and have them purified. Early in the morning he would sacrifice a burnt offering for each of them, thinking, "Perhaps my children have sinned and cursed God in their hearts." This was Job's regular custom.' (Job 1:2,4,5).

With such a wealthy father, Job's children could afford to enjoy an active social life. Family life is a great blessing, but it carries enormous responsibilities for the parents, especially in a godless age like ours. The point to notice is Job's balanced approach to his children. He loved them but did not idolise them. He did not deny them their pleasures and

Job's character and background

enjoyments, but at the same time he was not blind to their faults and the possibility of their falling into sin. He could not protect them indefinitely from the vicious influences of the world and its pleasures, so he created a counterbalance to any corruption that could spoil their lives by surrounding them with prayer. In short, he had a deep concern for the spiritual welfare of his children, and that is a powerful lesson for all Christian parents.

There is no task more difficult today than being a Christian parent. There are forces at work in our society that have the deliberate aim and intent of destroying our children's innocence and corrupting their souls. What is more, we must not think that our children are incapable of committing the grossest sins and lending themselves to the foulest practices. That would be totally unrealistic. The Psalmist was so right when he cried, 'Surely I was sinful at birth, sinful from the time my mother conceived me' (Psalm 51:5). Our children have to contend not only with the increase of evil in today's world but also with the down-drag of their own sinful nature. We have to nourish spiritual life in them, therefore, and guard them against the devil's attacks. This does not mean that we have to be heavy-handed as parents, denying them legitimate pleasures and enjoyments, but it does mean that we will not dilute the principles of the gospel in our family life, even if they do not like it. Obviously, we cannot control our children's lifestyle when they are outside the home but, like Job, we can pray for them continually. Praying is better than pressurising.

Job lived before the institution of the Levitical priesthood and its sacrificial system, and therefore as spiritual head of the family he acted as a priest, offering sacrifices for the expiation of his children's sins. The important thing to notice here is that 'This was Job's regular custom' (Job 1:5). That is, he was so concerned for the spiritual welfare of his children that he offered sacrifices daily on their behalf, or at least after every time they had been feasting in their homes. As Christian parents we have no need to make such repeated sacrifices, but we do have the responsibility to plead repeatedly the once-for-all sacrifice of our High Priest, the Lord Jesus Christ, for the atonement of sins, including those of our children. 'But when this priest had offered for all time one sacrifice for sins, he sat down at the right hand of God' (Hebrews 10:12).

Chapter 2

God's dialogue with Satan

Read Job 1:6–12

In this section the scene and situation changes from earth to heaven. A curtain is drawn aside, as it were, and we are allowed a glimpse into the very throne room of God, where a great assembly or council is taking place. 'One day the angels came to present themselves before the LORD, and Satan also came with them. The Lord said to Satan, "Where have you come from?" Satan answered the Lord, "From roaming through the earth and going to and fro in it"' (Job 1:6–7).

We can understand why the angels should be gathered in the presence of God. The Bible teaches that they are God's messengers engaged in his service: 'Are not all angels ministering spirits sent to serve those who will inherit salvation?' (Hebrews 1:14). Perhaps this picture of the angelic assembly is meant to teach us that periodically the angels are summoned into God's presence to report on errands and duties they have carried out. But it is more difficult to understand why Satan should be present. And yet we must not forget that he too is God's servant—an unwilling servant certainly, but still having to account to God for his doings. For it is clear from the dialogue which God initiates that whatever Satan does in this world can only be with God's permissive will.

Satan's activity

God begins the dialogue with a question. 'Where have you come from?' We must note here that whenever God asks a question in Scripture it is never for the purpose of obtaining information, least of all from Satan, because he already knows everything. But God asks questions in order to teach us something. In this instance the teaching concerns Satan's activity, and it comes out in his reply: 'From roaming through the earth and going to and fro in it.' This reminds us of Peter's description: 'Your enemy the devil prowls around like a roaring lion looking for someone to devour' (1 Peter 5:8). That seems to be Satan's main preoccupation, prowling and roaming the earth, like a restless lion seeking its prey. That is something we need to

God's dialogue with Satan

take on board, since there are those claiming to be Christians who accept the reality of sin and evil in the world but do not believe in the person of the devil.

The Scriptures are quite emphatic, however, that evil is not simply an abstract force or principle in the world but is personalised in Satan. The name 'Satan' means 'adversary' or 'one who opposes'. That is his whole aim and intention: to oppose God, his truth and his people. We are not dealing in the Christian life with any abstract principle of evil, but with a real malignant personality who plans and schemes as he roams the earth and has a definite strategy to hinder the work of God in his Church and people. The Lord Jesus gives a good example of this in his parable of the Sower and the preaching of God's Word. 'The seed is the word of God. Those along the path are the ones who hear, and then the devil comes and takes away the word from their hearts, so that they may not believe and be saved' (Luke 8:11–12). There is no suggestion here that evil is some kind of abstract principle. Rather, our Lord is saying that Satan is a personal intelligence whose deliberate strategy is to hinder the work of God's kingdom by preventing people from believing the word of the gospel. He also emphasises the personal existence of Satan by describing him as 'the prince of this world' (John 12:31) and as 'a liar and the father of lies' (John 8:44). The temptations through which our Lord passed in the wilderness (Matthew 4) were real because the tempter himself was real. He was no imaginary opponent but the 'prince of demons' (Matthew 9:34), who with implacable hatred gave battle to Christ the Messiah in order to destroy him and his kingdom. But Christ gained the supremacy and 'the devil left him'. As the 'ruler of the kingdom of the air' (Ephesians 2:2) Satan has under his command an army of demons engaged in a cosmic warfare with God's kingdom of truth and righteousness. But the victory over the kingdom of darkness has already been won at Calvary, although the final disposal of the devil and his fallen angels will not take place until time has ended, and Christ is raised 'far above all rule and authority, power and dominion' (Ephesians 1:21) and rules for all eternity.

His interest in believers

God takes the dialogue a step further. 'Have you considered my servant

Chapter 2

Job? There is no one on earth like him; he is blameless and upright, a man who fears God and shuns evil' (Job 1:8). Here again God's question is meant to teach us something about Satan's activity, the way that he pays special attention to believers. He had indeed considered Job very closely and knew all about him, as is evident from his reply. '"Does Job fear God for nothing?" Satan replied. "Have you not put a hedge around him and his household and everything he has? You have blessed the work of his hands so that his flocks and herds are spread throughout the land"' (Job 1:9–10). All who belong to the Lord Jesus Christ get the special attention of Satan. He watches us very closely, every move we make, examining every detail of our lives, assessing our strengths and weaknesses as he devises the best form of attack to bring us crashing down morally and spiritually. And when the time is right, he will strike just as he did with Job.

One of Satan's many strategies in attacking God's people is to use the weapon of accusation. In this instance he accuses Job of serving God out of self-interest. 'Does Job fear God for nothing?' In effect, he says to God, 'It is true that your servant Job is blameless and upright and shuns evil, but that is only because it pays him to live like that. He is acting out of self-interest, not because he loves you. You've guarded and protected him, put a hedge around him, so that his lifestyle is comfortable and easy. He has wealth and status and a happy family without any worries or problems, and that is why he serves you.' And then Satan goes further and challenges God on the basis of his accusation against Job: 'But stretch out your hand and strike everything he has, and he will surely curse you to your face' (Job 1:11). What an accusation! He is saying that Job's faith in God is no more than a thin veneer, and if he is exposed to the sharp edges of life his true self will be revealed, and it will be seen that he is as self-centred and self-serving as anyone else.

The accuser

In a vision given to the prophet Zechariah we have a picture similar to the one above, in which Satan accuses Joshua the high priest before the Lord. 'Then he showed me Joshua the high priest standing before the angel of the Lord, and Satan standing at his right side to accuse him' (Zechariah 3:1). And we read in Revelation, 'For the accuser of our brothers, who accuses them before our God day and night, has been hurled down' (Revelation

God's dialogue with Satan

12:10). Accusation is a definite strategy of Satan, and a very subtle device that he uses to great effect when other methods fail. He can attack a Christian by blatantly tempting him into some gross sin like sexual wickedness or stealing or cheating, only to find that it gets him nowhere. But then he changes his tactics and accuses him through the conscience, attacking his motives, pointing out his inner weaknesses, whispering that he is a hypocrite not worthy to be called a child of God. So the accusations go on, and they can have a crippling effect upon a person's Christian life where all else fails.

This was his strategy with Job, and the things he accuses him of must be looked at because they come a little too close to the truth for comfort. First, there is the accusation that our faith in God's mercy and goodness is real and genuine only when things are going well with us as they were with Job. When God puts a hedge around us, so to speak, so that our life is comfortable and undisturbed by problems or difficulties of any kind, then being faithful to our Christian convictions and praising God for his loving kindness is something that comes easily to us. But when the way is hard, when sickness and bereavement enter our home, when each day seems to bring with it new worries and added tensions, and the hedge seems to have been taken down, leaving the way open for Satan to attack—then our faith shrivels and we become resentful towards God. That is what Satan accuses us of as God's people. Is it true? Is our love for God based on a large measure of self-interest? Sadly, there is more than a grain of truth in the accusation. There are believers who, under the pressures of life, immediately take it out on God. They fall away from worship, give up on their prayer time and become cold in their devotion. It is an important question therefore: What happens when the hedge is taken down?

Second, implied in Satan's accusation is the implication that God's grace in our lives is an illusion. He challenges God directly with the words: 'But stretch out your hand and strike everything he has, and he will surely curse you to your face.' He is saying, in effect, that when we become believers through faith in Christ nothing happens to us on the inside of our lives, and it is a fantasy to believe that anything of God's nature and Spirit and power enters our hearts. Let the hedge be taken down, says Satan, and he will prove it. He is wrong, and we know it from our own experience of the power

Chapter 2

of God's grace in our lives. But, for the sake of his truth, God cannot allow the accusation to go unmet, and he accepts the challenge. 'The LORD said to Satan, "Very well, then, everything he has is in your hands, but on the man himself do not lay a finger." Then Satan went out from the presence of the Lord' (Job 1:12).

God took the hedge down from around Job and allowed Satan to attack him in order to prove the reality of his faith. Risky? You may think so, but God knew what he was doing and, more than that, he knew his man. His confidence was not in the strength of Job's faith, but in the strength of his own grace which had worked in Job's life and made him the man he was. That must surely be saying something very encouraging to us. When our lives are in turmoil and the troubles of this world come thick and fast upon us, we must remind ourselves of what is really taking place. God has taken down the hedge for a little while and is making our life a battleground: 'our struggle is ... against the powers of this dark world and against spiritual forces of evil in the heavenly realms' (Ephesians 6:12). There is a sense in which that is a great privilege. God is saying to Satan, 'I know my man, my woman.' There is a lot at stake: from our side, the reality of our faith in the Lord Jesus Christ, and from God's side, the reality of his saving grace in our lives. That grace did not fail Job, and it will not fail us. We have his promise that 'My grace is sufficient for you, for my power is made perfect in weakness' (2 Corinthians 12:9).

It may help us to understand more fully why God allowed Satan to attack Job through the trial of suffering if we keep in mind the nature of earthly trials. In the Bible trials have a double aspect. From Satan's side they are used as a temptation to seduce the believer into sin and disobedience to God's law. Satan does this by manipulating our earthly circumstances, as in Job's case, so that we will curse God and accuse him of treating us unfairly. But from God's side the same temptation is not an enticement to do what is evil, but a test intended to strengthen our faith so that he may use us more fully for his purposes. In one of his hymns John Newton describes an experience he had. He prayed that God would enable him to have a deeper faith and a greater knowledge of his love; but instead of answering his prayer in any positive way, God allowed his soul, for a period, to be assaulted by the very powers of hell itself.

God's dialogue with Satan

I asked the Lord that I might grow
In faith, and love, and every grace;
Might more of his salvation know,
And seek, more earnestly, his face.

I hoped that in some favored hour,
At once he'd answer my request;
And by his love's constraining pow'r,
Subdue my sins, and give me rest.

Instead of this, he made me feel
The hidden evils of my heart;
And let the angry pow'rs of hell
Assault my soul in every part.

'Lord, why is this', I trembling cried,
'Wilt thou pursue thy worm to death?'
''Tis in this way,' the Lord replied,
'I answer prayer for grace and faith.

'These inward trials I employ,
From self, and pride, to set thee free;
And break thy schemes of earthly joy,
That thou may'st find thy all in me.'

Chapter 3

The testing of Job

Read Job 1:13–2:10

Having been given permission by God to put Job's faith to the test, Satan launches his attack with bewildering ferocity and rapidity. The repetitive phrase 'While he was still speaking', used of the messengers who bring the bad news of Job's calamities, means not only that he was given no respite but that Satan was determined to bludgeon him into the ground. First, all the oxen and donkeys are stolen by marauding Sabean tribesmen, and Job's servants are put to the sword (Job 1:13–14). Then the flocks of sheep and the shepherds are destroyed by fire, possibly lightning (Job 1:16). This is followed by Chaldean raiding parties driving off the herds of camels (Job 1:17). And finally came the greatest disaster of all, when Job's whole family is wiped out by a tornado (Job 1:18–20).

Job's day of evil

All this must have left Job reeling with shock to his nervous system. I can recall speaking to an American couple who had experienced the destructive effects of an earthquake, and hearing them describe their feelings of utter desolation at the loss of their home and many of their prized possessions. What happened to Job was infinitely worse than that. He lost everything: his home, his livelihood and his family. But even that was not all. As we move into chapter 2 we find Satan once again before God in the presence of the angels.

Then the Lord said to Satan, 'Have you considered my servant Job? There is no one on earth like him; he is blameless and upright, a man who fears God and shuns evil. And he still maintains his integrity, though you incited me against him to ruin him without any reason.' 'Skin for skin!' Satan replied. 'A man will give all he has for his own life. But stretch out your hand and strike his flesh and bones, and he will surely curse you to your face.' The Lord said to Satan, 'Very well, then, he is in your hands; but you must spare his life.' So Satan went out from the presence of the Lord and afflicted Job with painful sores from the soles of his feet to the top of his head. Then Job took a piece of broken pottery and scraped himself with it as he sat among the ashes (Job 2:3–8).

This was certainly Job's 'day of evil', as Paul calls it in Ephesians 6:13, when the attack of Satan upon the child of God is especially concentrated and malevolent. We all have experiences of encountering evil and being faced with temptation, but there are times or days which are particularly evil, when we are acutely conscious of Satan's presence and feel that he has made us his special target and is determined to break us. That is how it was with Job. But although he was bewildered by the suddenness of it all and his emotions were in a state of turmoil, he was not bludgeoned into cursing God as Satan said he would. 'At this, Job got up and tore his robe and shaved his head' (Job 1:20). We can understand his deep expression of grief and mourning; that was perfectly natural. But he also did something else: 'Then he fell to the ground in worship and said: "Naked I came from my mother's womb, and naked I shall depart. The Lord gave and the Lord has taken away; may the name of the Lord be praised." In all this, Job did not sin by charging God with wrongdoing' (Job 1:20–22).

Believer and non-believer alike are subject to the trials and tragedies of this life, but there is a very real sense in which the suffering which calamities bring is of greater intensity for the Christian than for the secular man or woman. That is because, in addition to the physical and emotional pain, there is the inner 'writhing of the soul' as we question the integrity and faithfulness of God, and struggle to try and understand why he allows such devastation to come to his children. It is just here that we can learn from Job's response. In all that was happening to him he did not take his eye off God for a moment—'he fell to the ground in worship'. He did not understand what was happening to him, but neither did he do the one thing Satan wanted him to do: he 'did not sin by charging God with wrongdoing'. He was able to go even further, and to praise God for allowing him to enjoy for a time all those things—home, family and livelihood—which had now been taken from him. 'Naked I came from my mother's womb, and naked I shall depart.' What he is saying is that God owes him nothing. All that he possessed was held in stewardship for God. It will help us in our losses and suffering if we can remember that too, hard though it is. Satan may seek to rob us of everything—our health, family, livelihood—but if we keep our

Chapter 3

eye upon God, he cannot rob us of our salvation and our eternal security in the Lord Jesus Christ. Like Job, our response to life's trials will be to keep our wills submissive to the will of God and our hearts worshipful, whilst 'we fix our eyes not on what is seen, but on what is unseen. For what is seen is temporary, but what is unseen is eternal' (2 Corinthians 4:18). I am reminded here of the final verse in Luther's great hymn, 'A safe stronghold our God is still':

> God's Word, for all their craft and force,
> One moment will not linger,
> But, spite of hell, shall have its course;
> 'Tis written by His finger.
> And though they take our life,
> Goods, honour, children, wife,
> Yet is their profit small:
> These things shall vanish all;
> The city of God remaineth.

The limitations and extent of Satan's power

We are sometimes in danger of adopting one of two extremes where Satan's power is concerned. On the one hand we can overrate his power and treat him as if he were almost equal with God. He is not, for he is a created being and does not possess God's attributes of omnipotence, omniscience and omnipresence. The limits of his power may be seen in the fact that he can only do to Job what God directs and allows him to do. But even greater is the danger of underestimating his power, which is very extensive. The first two of his attacks upon Job are connected with his manipulation of men, the Sabeans and Chaldeans; the second two with his control over the forces of nature, the fire and wind; and the last one with his use of sickness in afflicting Job's body.

Whether he is aware of it or not, man, outside of God, is in collusion with Satan, who is described in Scripture as 'the prince of this world' (John 12:31) and the 'god of this age' (2 Corinthians 4:4). John further says that 'the whole world is under the control [*or better*, influence] of the evil one'

(1 John 5:19). Therefore, when the Sabean and Chaldean raiders carried off Job's flocks and herds and put his servants to the sword, they were being manipulated by Satan, who wields terrible power over the minds and wills of men. Immediately prior to his betrayal of Jesus we read, 'Then Satan entered Judas, called Iscariot' (Luke 22:3). This can only mean that he was under the influence of Satan. Even the Christian, at times, can become an unwitting instrument of Satan, as happened when Peter tried to deflect our Lord from the way of the cross and was told, 'Get behind me, Satan!' (Matthew 16:23). It is this Satanic energy expressing itself in the manipulation of men that is behind all the filth and immorality of our time. In his book *Satan Cast Out*, Frederick S Leahy makes the comment: 'Behind the dictators, the totalitarian systems, the persecuting powers, the capricious tyrants of this earth, the Bible sees Satan and his subalterns arrayed against mankind in general and the Church of God in particular.'

Satan, with the permissive will of God, can also at times have control over the forces of nature, which he utilises for his own evil purposes. The fire of God that destroyed Job's sheep may well have been lightning, and the mighty wind that destroyed the house of his children may well have been a tornado; but Satan had a hand in both. In the account of our Lord stilling the storm he rebukes the wind and the sea as if they were rational agents. This suggests that behind the restless elements he saw the hand of Satan in an attempt to destroy him: 'He got up, rebuked the wind and said to the waves, "Quiet! Be still!" Then the wind died down and it was completely calm' (Mark 4:39). This rebuke is almost identical to that given to the man possessed by an evil spirit at the beginning of Mark's Gospel: '"Be quiet!" said Jesus sternly. "Come out of him!"' (Mark 1:25). Satan's power is extensive, therefore, and can at times control the forces of nature to cause confusion and harm to the work and people of God.

Thirdly, Satan knows our human nature well and understands how highly we value bodily health and comfort. Sickness, therefore, can be a powerful instrument in his hands, and he used it with great effect upon Job. What a tragic sight Job presents, sitting among the ashes and seeking relief from his pain by scraping the revolting sores that disfigured his emaciated body 'from the soles of his feet to the top of his head'! (Job 2:7–8). And it was all Satan's doing, in an attempt to break his faith. We recall Paul's

Chapter 3

explanation for what he calls his thorn in the flesh, describing it as 'a messenger of Satan, to torment me' (2 Corinthians 12:7). Another example of Satanic bodily affliction is given by the Lord Jesus when he said of a crippled woman: 'Then should not this woman … whom Satan has kept bound for eighteen long years, be set free …?' (Luke 13:16). It is a fearful thought that Satan can have a direct hand in attacking our bodies, with the purpose of lowering our spirit and estranging us from God. He attempted it with Job but failed to get him to curse God.

And we likewise must determine that he will fail with us in our time of sickness. To help us in that, we must hold fast to the doctrine of God's sovereignty. For all his sinister power and cunning, Satan is a created being, and therefore no match for the sovereign God who created him. He is the enemy of our souls, and he will use every means at his disposal to bring about our destruction. But we must never forget that he is a defeated enemy, and that all his vicious attacks upon the believer are but a counter-offensive against the crushing defeat he received at Calvary. What is more, it is a counter-offensive that is doomed to failure. He cannot harm believers, because we belong to Christ and his victory is our victory. We are the 'overcomers' of whom John speaks in his letter: 'for everyone born of God overcomes the world. This is the victory that has overcome the world, even our faith. Who is it that overcomes the world? Only he who believes that Jesus is the Son of God' (1 John 5:4–5).

Job's wife

We said earlier that Satan manipulates men for his own evil purposes. That comes out clearly in the response of Job's wife to all that had happened to him. '"Are you still holding on to your integrity? Curse God and die!" He replied, "You are talking like a foolish woman. Shall we accept good from God, and not trouble?" In all this Job did not sin in what he said' (Job 2:9–10).

Satan will stoop to anything, and use any means to undermine the faith of God's people. He will use even our own family, husband, wife or children, to achieve his ends. The response of Job's wife also teaches us how subtle temptation can be, and how Satan can approach us as an angel of light. It is not always those who are hostile to the gospel who cause us harm;

it may be those who love us dearly and have our best interests at heart. Unwittingly perhaps, Job's wife becomes Satan's mouthpiece and urges him to do the very thing Satan wanted him to do, to 'Curse God and die!' It could be that it was love for her husband that led her to feel that it was better for him to end his life than continue in such misery. But Job would have none of it, as his reply makes clear: 'Shall we accept good from God, and not trouble?' This matches the spirit of Romans 8:28—'And we know that in all things God works for the good of those who love him, who have been called according to his purpose.' Job had enjoyed many of the good things of this life, and now that adversity and trial had come to him he is prepared to accept that too as coming from God, and submits to his will. 'In all this Job did not sin in what he said' (Job 1:10). At this point he 'accepts' without question that God is in absolute control of his life and that his suffering is in no way a sign that God has forsaken him. God is just and righteous, he believes, and therefore he accepts without murmuring all that has happened to him. Later, as we shall see, he is not so reticent in questioning God's dealings with him and has plenty of hard things to say about his goodness and justice. But we must not be too hard on Job. For we ourselves, whilst we accept the sovereignty of God in the control he exercises over our lives, nevertheless find it difficult in the time of suffering and trial to accept that 'in all things God works for the good of those who love him'. Yet it is true! All things do work harmoniously for the believer within the marvellous providence of God, for we 'have been called according to his purpose'. That purpose is to bring us to glory, and no amount of suffering or trial, however intense or severe, can prevent us from entering into the joy and blessedness of heaven.

Chapter 4

Job's lament

Read Job 2:11–3:26

This section opens with Job's friends coming to comfort him when they hear of his distress. 'When Job's three friends, Eliphaz the Temanite, Bildad the Shuhite and Zophar the Naamathite, heard about all the troubles that had come upon him, they set out from their homes and met together by agreement to go and sympathise with him and comfort him' (Job 2:11). We have all heard the expression 'Job's comforter' used when we aggravate the distress of someone with depressing advice. But this is not altogether fair to Job's friends. As we shall see, the advice they gave was not always the best advice (although they spoke a lot of sense too) and they were also critical of Job at times, but in no way were they malicious or vindictive. What is more, they did show true friendship by going to the trouble of visiting Job, and when they saw him they were genuinely distressed at his appearance and expressed their condolences in the traditional way. 'When they saw him from a distance, they could hardly recognise him; they began to weep aloud, and they tore their robes and sprinkled dust on their heads' (Job 2:12).

That is what true friendship is at the spiritual level: it is weeping with those who weep and identifying with them in their suffering and trial. We read: 'Then they sat on the ground with him for seven days and seven nights. No-one said a word to him, because they saw how great his suffering was' (Job 2:13). There are situations in this life when words seem to be entirely inadequate, since we would only be stating the obvious or making the most banal comments. Therefore it is better to remain silent. As the Scriptures remind us, there is 'a time to be silent and a time to speak' (Ecclesiastes 3:7). But what undoubtedly helped and comforted Job was simply the warmth of their presence and the fact that they cared. This real affection he had for them comes out at the end of the book, when he intercedes for them in prayer to God to forgive them for the wrong things they had said about him (Job 42:8). In the time of stress, bereavement and trial it is not always words that are important in the first instance, but just the fact that someone cares and is willing to identify with us in sharing the burden.

That comes close to the heart of the gospel. The Lord Jesus said of those who believe in him, 'You are my friends if you do what I command' (John 15:14). We are the objects of his special love and friendship. He identifies with us in all our need and suffering and shares our burdens.

A cry from the heart

For seven days Job and his friends had sat in silence, but during that time he had been thinking and pondering deeply on all that happened to him, and now he gives vent to his feelings in what is a true cry from the heart. 'After this Job opened his mouth and cursed the day of his birth. He said: "May the day of my birth perish, and the night it was said, 'A boy is born!' That day, may it turn to darkness … May darkness and deep shadow claim it once more; may a cloud settle over it; may blackness overwhelm its light"' (Job 3:1–5). He continues speaking in the same pathetic strain down to verse 12, lamenting the fact that he had ever been born. All he can see ahead is further pain and loneliness.

What we have here in the first instance is the picture of a man experiencing profound emotional conflict and sunk in deep depression. Many of us will sympathise with him because we may have had occasion to feel the same way. Suffering can do that to you; it can make you act out of character and say things under the impulse of the moment that you do not really mean. Elijah felt the same depressing sense of hopelessness when he fled to the wilderness and prayed that he might die: '"I have had enough, Lord," he said. "Take my life; I am no better than my ancestors"' (1 Kings 19:4). Jeremiah, hurt and depressed in the face of resentment and ridicule, cried: 'Cursed be the day I was born! May the day my mother bore me not be blessed!' (Jeremiah 20:14). We cannot justify such an outburst even in godly men like Job, Elijah and Jeremiah, but we can understand it, because it reflects our own experience. The question is, Should we, as Christian believers, be ashamed of such feelings? I do not think so, because it is a part of our God-given humanity. We are not machines or robots, but we have emotions and feelings capable of being hurt by the harsh realities of life. We need to remember that, because there are some Christians who feel guilty

Chapter 4

when they become depressed and think within themselves, 'I shouldn't feel like this. I'm a child of God, and this is wrong.' But such thinking only aggravates the condition. The truth is that different factors can contribute to our depressed state of mind, such as sickness or personal temperament. The important thing is to handle it in the right way.

Escaping the realities

When it comes to dealing with our low depressed spirit, perhaps the greatest mistake we can make is to dwell on it and to allow Satan to exploit it to the point where it becomes an obsession. Wallowing in it will lead us into a state of morbidity, defeatism and despair. That is when the depressive mood becomes wrong and sinful for the Christian. We are then making our feelings central, whereas what should be central at all times is the great truth of God himself, that he is there even in the darkest moments. Job seems to have forgotten this in the midst of the enormous stress he was under, and he had given way to such despair that his one thought was to withdraw from life itself and to avoid facing up to its realities. He wanted a way of escape.

He wishes he had never been born and asks, 'Why did I not perish at birth, and die as I came from the womb? Why were there knees to receive me and breasts that I might be nursed?' (Job 3:11–12). But the fact was that he *had* been born and he had no choice in the matter; it was an unavoidable reality of life that he simply had to accept, whether he liked it or not. And it is like that with us. Apart from those times when, through our own stupidity and sinfulness, we do ourselves a disservice, most of the pressures and burdens of this life cannot be avoided and we just have to learn to accept them. But the impulse to want to escape from the pressures of life is strong within us, and it is only through the strength and power God gives that we can overcome it. Even the Psalmist had to learn that: 'My heart is in anguish within me; the terrors of death assail me. Fear and trembling have beset me; horror has overwhelmed me. I said, "Oh that I had the wings of a dove! I would fly away and be at rest—I would flee far away and stay in the desert; I would hurry to my place of shelter, far from the tempest and storm"' (Psalm 55:4–8). But he discovered that escape from the realities of life was not the answer, and that he could in fact bear his burden with the

Job's lament

help of God, for he ends on the positive note: 'Cast your cares on the Lord and he will sustain you; he will never let the righteous fall' (Psalm 55:22). And Peter is equally positive when he says: 'Cast all your anxiety on him because he cares for you' (1 Peter 5:7).

All this, of course, heightens the pitiable and tragic state of the non-Christian in the face of the dark side of life. He has no faith in the caring, loving God to help him accept it, and he says to himself, 'I didn't ask to be born into this rotten world, but at least I don't have to accept it.' He then comes up with his own form of escapism. He may turn to the bottle and drown himself in the bleary world of alcohol, or escape into the fantasy world of drugs. The workaholic buries himself in his career, to the exclusion of everything else; the hypochondriac seeks refuge in illness, imaginary or otherwise; and the pleasure-lover loses himself or herself in a ceaseless round of activities and social engagements or love affairs, in order to shut out the harsh realities and demands of each day.

But none of these work, for life in the end, however harsh and demanding, has to be faced. Or has it? This is the other sad thing we notice in Job's lament: his view of death as the final escape route.

Death the ultimate escape?

Having expressed his wish that he had never been born, Job, in an even more morbid frame of mind, longs for death as the final rest from all his troubles. 'For now I would be lying down in peace; I would be asleep and at rest with kings and counsellors of the earth, who built for themselves places now lying in ruins, with rulers who had gold, who filled their houses with silver' (Job 3:13–15). He continues in the same vein: 'There the wicked cease from turmoil, and there the weary are at rest. Captives also enjoy their ease; they no longer hear the slave driver's shout. The small and the great are there, and the slave is freed from his master. Why is light given to those in misery, and life to the bitter of soul, to those who long for death that does not come, who search for it more than for hidden treasure, who are filled with gladness and rejoice when they reach the grave?' (Job 3:17–22).

It is sad, to our Christian understanding, to hear a godly man like Job speak of death in this confused way—as something to be welcomed by all,

Chapter 4

for then one is at peace and set free from all earthly burdens; the ultimate escape for great and small, when the prince and the slave, and even the wicked, cease from their turmoil and are at ease. But we should not be too critical of Job, for he did not enjoy the full light of truth in relation to death and the after-life that we have in the revelation of Christ. Therefore he is wrong, absolutely wrong, from the standpoint of the gospel—and so are all those today who think that death is an annihilation, a deep dreamless sleep that puts an end to all earthly troubles and trials. That is the tragedy of the thousands every year in this country, the majority of them young people, who deliberately seek death as the ultimate escape from the burdens of life. For the Bible teaches consistently that death is not a dreamless sleep or a state of non-existence, but it brings us into the presence of the eternal God, to whom we have to give an account: 'man is destined to die once, and after that to face judgment' (Hebrews 9:27). That surely is the most dreadful reality of all, and there is no escaping it for the person who on earth has lived outside the mercy and forgiveness of God in Jesus Christ.

In defence of Job we must make allowance for the fact that he was speaking out of a deeply troubled spirit. He realised later how foolish and impulsive his words had been: 'If only my anguish could be weighed and all my misery be placed on the scales! It would surely outweigh the sand of the seas—no wonder my words have been impetuous' (Job 6:2–3). And later still, when he again speaks of death, he does so in words that breathe the very spirit of the gospel of Christ: 'I myself will see him with my own eyes—I, and not another. How my heart yearns within me!' (Job 19:27). That is the Christian view of death: something to be yearned for, not as an escape from the realities of life, but as an entrance into the eternal reality of God's loving presence.

Chapter 5

Yesterday's testimony, today's blessing

Read Job chapters 4 and 5

Eliphaz, one of the friends, has listened quietly and respectfully to Job's lament, and in this and the next chapter he makes his own thoughts known. 'Then Eliphaz the Temanite replied: "If someone ventures a word with you, will you be impatient? But who can keep from speaking?"' (Job 4:1–2). He has no wish to be offensive, and yet at the same time, because Job has said some shocking things, like expressing a wish to die, Eliphaz feels he must speak his mind openly and honestly. 'Think how you have instructed many, how you have strengthened feeble hands. Your words have supported those who stumbled; you have strengthened faltering knees. But now trouble comes to you, and you are discouraged; it strikes you, and you are dismayed. Should not your piety be your confidence and your blameless ways your hope?' (Job 4:3–6).

Past faithfulness

Eliphaz gives a glowing testimony to Job's past faithfulness in the things of God. He had always exercised a real ministry of encouragement, giving guidance and instruction and helping those in distress. God had used him greatly. Job knows in his heart that this is true, because later on, when reflecting on happier days when he had his health and family and prosperity, he spells out the positive life he had led and how he was able in his position to help so many. 'The man who was dying blessed me; I made the widow's heart sing. I put on righteousness as my clothing; justice was my robe and my turban. I was eyes to the blind and feet to the lame. I was a father to the needy; I took up the case of the stranger' (Job 29:13–15). This was not boasting, but a simple recognition of the fact that God had blessed him and he was able to use his wealth and position to glorify God in what he did for others.

Chapter 5

We can all learn from Job's example, even if we do not have wealth and an influential position. In his list of gifts given to the local church in Romans 12, Paul mentions such simple, ordinary things as 'serving', 'encouraging', 'contributing to the needs of others' and 'showing mercy'. These are things God can use in the local fellowship, and they do not require wealth, special talent or social standing. And we can exercise them in many ways, through praying regularly for someone, writing to a missionary on a regular basis, getting alongside a new convert, expressing a word of appreciation and encouragement. In all these ways we can 'strengthen feeble hands, support those who stumble, and strengthen faltering knees' (Job 4:3–4).

Present blessings

Having testified to Job's past faithfulness, Eliphaz nevertheless points out that he is not living up to that testimony in the present. 'But now trouble comes to you, and you are discouraged; it strikes you, and you are dismayed. Should not your piety be your confidence and your blameless ways your hope?' (Job 4:5–6). The question Eliphaz asks is, Where is that glowing testimony to God's blessing now? And he touches on three home truths that have relevance to us.

First, none of us can live on our past experience of God's blessing and power in our lives, but we must know it in the present. There are Christians who are always talking about what God has done *for* them and *in* them in the past. They are always relating yesterday's experience. That is perfectly all right as far as it goes, but the question is, Is God using us and blessing us today? Have we moved on with God in Christ? Is our experience of his salvation richer now than it was twenty or thirty years ago? Is our zeal for God and the gospel greater? Are we more faithful now than we were then?

Second, we can fail to apply to our own personal situations in life the teaching and witness we have faithfully given to others. Eliphaz tells Job that he had always encouraged others in God, but now that trouble comes to him he is filled with discouragement and dismay. Is that true of us? Have we comforted others in the gospel and encouraged them to stand firm, and then, when trial has come to us, gone to pieces? Does that mean that our preaching and witness were just words and no more?

Third, where does our confidence really lie? Is it in God? Eliphaz reminds Job that it was his belief in the integrity of God that had given him confidence and steadfastness in the face of life in the past, and that this should be his confidence now, for although his circumstances have changed, God has not changed. That is true. Our situation may change and we may find ourselves dragged through the most testing of trials, but God is the same and his promises are the same. That is where our confidence must lie: not in ourselves, not in our friends or in the things we surround ourselves with, but in God.

Sin and suffering

Eliphaz now shifts his ground and becomes a bit more critical of Job, implying that, godly though he is, there must be some hidden sin in his life to account for the suffering he is having to endure. 'Consider now: Who, being innocent, has ever perished? Where were the upright ever destroyed? As I have observed, those who plough evil and those who sow trouble reap it. At the breath of God they are destroyed; at the blast of his anger they perish' (Job 4:7–9). He then gives an illustration to make his point more clearly. 'The lions may roar and growl, yet the teeth of the great lions are broken. The lion perishes for lack of prey, and the cubs of the lioness are scattered' (Job 4:10–11). The king of beasts, for all his strength, becomes old and toothless, and the cubs suffer from lack of food. In the same way the sin of the wicked, sooner or later, brings about the suffering and punishment of God.

Eliphaz was wrong in all this. It is not only sinful, wicked people who suffer in this life. The Bible is full of instances of godly folk who endured the most dreadful sufferings. Abel, a righteous man (Matthew 23:35), was the first person to be murdered (Genesis 4:8). Hebrews 11 gives a harrowing picture of the sufferings of the righteous: 'Some faced jeers and flogging, while still others were chained and put in prison. They were stoned; they were sawn in two; they were put to death by the sword. They went about in sheepskins and goatskins, destitute, persecuted and ill-treated … They wandered in deserts and mountains, and in caves and holes in the ground' (Hebrews 11:36–38). And what of all those who have been tortured, imprisoned and martyred for the Christian faith in our own time under

Chapter 5

totalitarian regimes? Besides, we already know the secret that it is not true of Job that he was being punished for his sins (Job 1:8; 2:3).

Eliphaz made the profound mistake of failing to distinguish between suffering because of deliberate sin and wickedness, and suffering because of righteousness. Or, to put it another way, people may suffer because they are sinful and as a judgement of God. But people may also suffer because they are saints, and, as in the case of Job, God uses their holiness of life under pressure as a form of witness and to glorify himself. Paul goes even further than that and says that by our sufferings we can help to fulfil the eternal purpose of God in the cross of Christ. 'Now I rejoice in what was suffered for you, and I fill up in my flesh what is still lacking in regard of Christ's afflictions, for the sake of his body, which is the church' (Colossians 1:24). When we suffer for the sake of the gospel we are, in some mystical way, helping to 'fill up' or 'complete' the purposes of God in bringing salvation to mankind. If we can see our sufferings in this way, it will not only make it more bearable but also meaningful, because we are glorifying God in it all.

How God speaks to us

In the final section of this chapter Eliphaz relates a strange and wonderful experience in which God spoke to him, and which was the inspiration for the advice and instruction he was giving Job. 'A word was secretly brought to me, my ears caught a whisper of it. Amid disquieting dreams in the night, when deep sleep falls on men, fear and trembling seized me and made all my bones shake. A spirit glided past my face … and I heard a hushed voice: "Can a mortal be more righteous than God? Can a man be more pure than his Maker?"' (Job 4:12–17).

We ought to be careful not to dismiss all talk of dreams and visions as being fanciful, and no more than a person's own subjective and speculative experience. The Scriptures give many instances when God spoke to men through dreams and visions. Joseph had two dreams in which his future was foretold, and later he was used of God to interpret the dreams of the butler and baker in prison, and of the reigning Pharaoh. God spoke to Jacob in a dream at Bethel, and through a dream gave the gift of wisdom to Solomon. In the New Testament God spoke to Joseph in a dream about the birth of Jesus, and Peter was asleep on the roof of the house when he received his dream (or vision) concerning Cornelius and the conversion of the Gentiles. Referring to his own remarkable experience Paul says he could not be sure if God spoke to him in a dream ('in the body') or in a vision ('out of the body') concerning things he could not talk about. And there are scores of instances outside of the Scriptures of the same spiritual phenomenon. One of the greatest Welsh preachers, Christmas Evans, said that it was in a dream that God called him to the preaching ministry. It is true that dreams and visions are no longer the norm whereby God reveals his will to us, since we now have the complete canon of Scripture, and the fullness of divine revelation in the person of the Lord Jesus Christ. But that is not to deny that God can still speak a personal word to us in any way he chooses, and if he cannot get through to us in our waking moments because our lives are so cluttered up with other things, then he will disturb our sleep. The important thing is to keep ourselves open and sensitive to the movement of the Holy Spirit, so that if God should speak to us, we will not miss it or doubt that he has in fact spoken. And it is also important to keep all such experiences subject to the Word of God.

Man's mortality

One of the truths revealed to Eliphaz in his dream concerned man's mortality. 'Can a mortal be more righteous than God? Can a man be more pure than his Maker?' The answer to both questions is clearly no. But Eliphaz was wrong to conclude that because mortal man is sinful he has no right to question, as Job does, God's dealings with him. God does not mind our questioning of his ways, provided that we do it with a humble heart and are prepared in the meantime to accept his ways until answers may be forthcoming. The Psalmist said, 'he knows how we are formed, he remembers that we are dust' (Psalm 103:14). God knows the limitations of our humanity, for he created us, and asking questions is a part of that limitation. But Eliphaz is right to remind Job of our mortality and the fragility of human life. He uses several figures of speech to ram the point home. Man lives in a house of clay. In the way you and I can crush a moth, so God can crush us (Job 4:19). Like a clay earthenware pot, man's life breaks down, his body crumbles, his intellectual powers wane, until eventually he

Chapter 5

dies forgotten and unnoticed (Job 4:20). Like the collapse of a tent when the cords are pulled up, so man leaves this world, and his so-called wisdom or cleverness cannot prevent it happening.

In the light of such fragility and brevity, therefore, how foolish modern man is to think that he has no need of the righteousness of God in Christ, and that his own wisdom and cleverness are sufficient to enable him to deal with all the issues of this earthly life!

Resentment towards God

As we move into chapter 5 Eliphaz continues to remonstrate with Job over his resentment and anger towards God because of what has happened to him. 'Call if you will, but who will answer you? To which of the holy ones will you turn? Resentment kills a fool, and envy slays the simple' (Job 5:1–2). He says in effect, 'If you feel so resentful because of what has happened to you, which of the "holy ones" [angels] will you appeal to for support in your cause against God? No, Job, you must learn that being resentful towards God is both foolish and wrong, because in the end the only one to get hurt is yourself.' He then goes on, 'I myself have seen a fool taking root, but suddenly his house was cursed. His children are far from safety, crushed in court without a defender. The hungry consume his harvest, taking it even from among thorns, and the thirsty pant after his wealth' (Job 5:3–5). He means that a wicked, morally degenerate person, hostile to God, may flourish like a plant in the earth, but at some point judgement will come, either in this life or the next.

Do we ever get angry with God? Someone has called it 'the pot-boiling syndrome', when we build up a head of steam on the inside. As a young man I remember I used to let off steam against God when things went wrong. I would get all churned up on the inside and fume against him because he was not being fair. As I got older in years and in faith, I learned the truth of what Eliphaz is saying. Getting angry with God is both foolish and counter-productive, since the only one to get hurt is oneself; it makes one morose and bitter. We certainly do not hurt God, so it is all a waste of spiritual energy.

In the first place we cannot influence God by being resentful towards him. We cannot, by our anger, browbeat God or manipulate him into doing what we want, in the way a little child gets its own way with mum by working up a tantrum. In the second place, getting angry with God is wrong and foolish, because it implies that we have rights and privileges where God is concerned and that he is obligated to take account of those rights in his dealings with us. But that is a nonsense! When Jonah got angry with God, what did God say to him? 'Have you any right to be angry?' (Jonah 4:4)—and the question is repeated in verse 9. In our society today everybody seems to be demanding his or her 'rights'. There may be a case for that in human society, but where God is concerned we have no rights, none at all. He owes us nothing. All that we have and are is due to his free mercy and grace in the Lord Jesus Christ. So let us resist the pot-boiling syndrome, for it gets us nowhere. We can plead with God, request of God, ask questions of God, and we can get somewhere. But the one thing we cannot do with a hope of achieving anything is to get angry with God. It is wrong and totally counter-productive, and a person is a fool to engage in it.

Resting in God's infinity

Eliphaz has been rather hard on Job, but from verse 8 to the end of the chapter his tone softens. He urges Job to stop haranguing God and instead to humbly rest in his infinity. After all, God is great and knows best. 'But if it were I, I would appeal to God; I would lay my cause before him. He performs wonders that cannot be fathomed, miracles that cannot be counted. He bestows rain on the earth; he sends water upon the countryside' (Job 5:8–10). He continues in this wonderful poetic vein down to verse 16, reminding Job that God is great and merciful: 'The lowly he sets on high, and those who mourn are lifted to safety' (Job 5:11). Isn't Eliphaz right in all this? When life is hard and difficult, instead of demanding explanations from God out of our bitterness of soul, it is far more comforting and helpful to rest in his infinite wisdom and love. The other writers of the Bible confirm the rightness of this attitude: 'those who hope in the LORD will renew their strength. They will soar on wings like eagles; they will run and not grow weary, they will walk and not be faint' (Isaiah 40:31). And Peter says, 'Humble yourselves, therefore, under God's mighty hand, that he may lift you up in due time. Cast all your anxiety on him because he cares for you' (1 Peter 5:6–7). Eliphaz had said earlier, 'Yet man

Chapter 5

is born to trouble as surely as sparks fly upward' (Job 5:7). That is true. Therefore, since trouble comes to us all, I would rather meet it with God than without him.

God's discipline

Can suffering and trial, even of the innocent, ever be positive and constructive? Eliphaz may not believe that Job is innocent of sin, but he certainly asserts that God uses suffering to discipline and refine our character, and to teach us to walk by faith and not by sight. 'Blessed is the man whom God corrects; so do not despise the discipline of the Almighty. For he wounds, but he also binds up; he injures, but his hands also heal' (Job 5:17–18). In the rest of this section, down to the end of the chapter, he tells Job that God will ultimately bring him through the darkness into the light of a new day. This was indeed prophetic, for as we know, Job did come through his sufferings triumphantly.

Life may bruise and batter us, but we hold on to the truth that in it all God has our ultimate good and welfare at heart.

Chapter 6

Self-justification and self-pity

Read Job chapters 6 and 7

In these two chapters Job replies to Eliphaz, who has taken him to task because of his resentment towards God, and we shall see that his anger has not been placated in any way. Indeed he even tries to justify his angry words.

Self-justification

These two chapters are full of word-pictures that need to be explained to get at the truth underlying them. 'Then Job replied: "If only my anguish could be weighed and all my misery be placed on the scales! It would surely outweigh the sand of the seas—no wonder my words have been impetuous"' (Job 6:1–3). The picture is of a pair of scales; Job has placed his sufferings on one side of the scales and his resentful words on the other, and it can easily be seen which is the heavier. He says in effect: 'No wonder my words are angry and impetuous! Who can blame me? Am I not justified in blaming God and feeling resentful?' And he then gives other pictures to justify his feelings. 'The arrows of the Almighty are in me, my spirit drinks in their poison' (Job 6: 4). God is the great hunter, and Job is his target. 'God has his hooks in me' is what he is saying. 'Does a wild donkey bray when it has grass, or an ox bellow when it has fodder?' (Job 6:5). For him to bellow and bray against God is perfectly in order, since he is being treated like an animal that is denied food. Indeed, the food [treatment] God has given him is as tasteless and insipid as the white of an egg (Job 6:6–7).

We may feel inclined to blame Job for his attempt at self-justification in God's sight, but in fact we ourselves are doing it in all sorts of ways. We find it hard to have a quiet time for prayer and reading God's Word, and we say to him, 'You know how rushed I am during the day, what with taking the children to school and then my work—and by the time I get home I'm too tired to take it in.' Or we may not wish to go to a worship service or week-night prayer meeting, and we come up with half a dozen reasons to convince ourselves that it will be far better for our spirit if we do the other

From despair to hope **39**

Chapter 6

thing that we intended doing all along. Or again, as we wrestle with the question of how much money we should give to God's work, we easily prove to ourselves that it is perfectly in order to cut down the amount because of other things that make a legitimate demand upon our limited resources. Psychology calls this the 'rationalisation of desire'. That is, we desire something and we rationalise or justify to our own satisfaction why we should have it. When we do this with God, it becomes much more serious, for then it is what Wesley in one of his hymns calls 'the arguments of sin'.

This is spiritually dangerous because, if we are not careful, we can justify in God's sight even our sins; and the things we once dreaded with shame because we knew they would grieve the Holy Spirit we find ourselves doing without a qualm. Furthermore, by justifying in God's sight the things contrary to his Word we are calling God a liar. We are saying that *we* have got it right and God has got it all wrong. But Paul says, 'Let God be true, and every man a liar' (Romans 3:4).

A sense of hopelessness

In this next section (verses 8–13) we sense the cloud of gloom that has descended on Job. 'Oh, that I might have my request, that God would grant what I hope for, that God would be willing to crush me, to let loose his hand and cut me off! Then I would still have this consolation—my joy in unrelenting pain—that I had not denied the words of the Holy One.' If this is a prayer, then it is a prayer of total unrelieved despair and hopelessness. Indeed he goes on to say as much: 'What strength do I have, that I should still hope? ... Do I have any power to help myself, now that success has been driven from me?'

There is no doubt that at times life can give us such a hammering that every vestige of hope can be drained from us. And then we are tempted to say to God, as Job does in verse 12, 'Do I have the strength of stone? Is my flesh bronze?' We are not supermen and superwomen, so how can we be expected to be hopeful and positive in what is a hopeless situation? But that is just it. From the biblical perspective there are no hopeless situations; there are only hopeless people in those situations. That surely is the difference between the Christian's hope in Christ and the false superficial optimism of the non-

Self-justification and self-pity

Christian. Job asks, 'Do I have any power to help myself, now that success has been driven from me?' (Job 6:13). There he is touching on the basic weakness of the worldly person. They have only their own power to rely on in the face of life's struggles, and since that is pretty weak at the best of times we can understand why they succumb to feelings of despair and hopelessness. We all need a power outside of ourselves and greater than our own. And that is what the gospel of Jesus Christ gives us. That power of God that brought the light and hope of the resurrection out of the despair and hopelessness of Calvary becomes our power and our hope.

Failure in friendship

In the final verses of chapter 6 (14–30) we come a little closer to Job and can understand how hurt he feels with his friends. 'A despairing man should have the devotion of his friends, even though he forsakes the fear of the Almighty. But my brothers are as undependable as intermittent streams, as the streams that overflow when darkened by thawing ice and swollen with melting snow, but that cease to flow in the dry season, and in the heat vanish from their channels … The caravans of Tema look for water … they arrive there, only to be disappointed. Now you too have proved to be of no help.'

The pictures here are of a friendship that is like a cold icy stream, lacking warmth and understanding, or a stream in the desert that dries up, disappointing the travelling caravans when they come to drink. He ends by telling his friends that he had not lied when he told them he was not guilty of sin and wrongdoing, but they had not believed him, and that is what he found so hurtful. 'But now be so kind as to look at me. Would I lie to your face? Relent, do not be unjust; reconsider, for my integrity is at stake' (verses 28–29). Eliphaz had spoken some basic fundamental truths that Job needed to hear, but it was the manner in which he had spoken that wounded Job. All the time he was implying that Job had committed some great sin, and when he denied it he questioned his integrity.

Within the Christian fellowship we must never avoid standing for the truth and speaking the truth, even at the risk of causing offence. If a fellow believer has to be rebuked for some sin or wrongdoing, then we must do it. But it is always 'speaking the truth in love' (Ephesians 4:15), and not in a chilling censorious manner which can be so hurtful.

Chapter 6

A hard life

As we move into chapter 7 Job is still in a deeply pessimistic mood, and this comes out clearly in the first eleven verses. 'Does not man have hard service on earth? Are not his days like those of a hired man? Like a slave longing for the evening shadows, or a hired man waiting eagerly for his wages, so I have been allotted months of futility, and nights of misery have been assigned to me' (Job 7:1–3). Life is hard, brutish and short, Job is saying, and he is convinced that he will never again know true happiness in the service of God. 'Remember, O God, that my life is but a breath; my eyes will never see happiness again. The eye that now sees me will see me no longer; you will look for me, but I will be no more' (Job 7:7–8). He ends this section determined to have his say: 'Therefore I will not keep silent … I will complain in the bitterness of my soul' (Job 7:11).

We sympathise with Job in the light of all he has gone through. But somehow we wish that, as a child of God, he could have found it in him to say something different, such as 'Well, I've lost everything else, but I've still got my faith in a loving and caring God.' It is not easy to say that when life has beaten you to your knees, but if anyone can say it, it has to be the child of God, for he alone has discovered that true happiness and contentment flow from the inside out, and not from the outside in. The secular man who complains 'It's a hard life' thinks he can change it into the good satisfying life by juggling things around a bit. If he were to get a job that was less boring and better paid, or change the house for something a bit bigger, or move into a better area where the neighbours were less noisy, then everything would be just perfect.

But it is all a pathetic illusion. If you look at the expert jugglers today— the showbiz people, television personalities and pop stars, who have got themselves into the seemingly perfect situation with fame and fortune— you will find that many of them have not found the satisfaction and contentment they are looking for. But then you can look at a Christian like Corrie ten Boom and her experiences in the Second World War. She was certainly not able to juggle things into the perfect situation; on the contrary, life had juggled her into a satanic situation in the Ravensbruck concentration camp, where she was surrounded by filth, starvation and death, and endured hours of cold and fatigue standing on meaningless parades. But in it all her contentment and sufficiency in Christ shone through. There is a saying, 'You can't make a good omelette with bad eggs.' You can juggle them around in the pan as much as you like, but it will still be a bad omelette. God made us for himself, and without him at the centre all the other ingredients we pour into our lives will never finally satisfy. Job was having to learn that lesson the hard way, but he did learn it eventually. Some of us have yet to learn it.

A distorted view of God

Pain and suffering can distort and twist everything, even our understanding of God. In these final verses (Job 7:12–21) Job pictures God as some sort of celestial tyrant or bully, intent on making him squirm. 'Am I the sea, or the monster of the deep, that you put me under guard? When I think my bed will comfort me and my couch will ease my complaint, even then you frighten me with dreams and terrify me with visions, so that I prefer strangling and death, rather than this body of mine. I despise my life; I would not live for ever. Let me alone; my days have no meaning' (verses 12–16). He accuses God of treating him like an animal or monster, to be tamed and kept under close surveillance. 'Let me alone,' he complains, or as we would say, 'Get off my back.' He pursues this theme of God the manwatcher scrutinising his every action. 'What is man that you make so much of him, that you give him so much attention, that you examine him every morning and test him every moment? Will you never look away from me, or let me alone even for an instant? If I have sinned, what have I done to you, O watcher of men?' (Job 7:17–20).

But in his anguish Job's picture of God is a complete distortion. 'What is man that you make so much of him?' he asks, thinking that God takes advantage of man's smallness and weakness and wants to impress upon him his insignificance and worthlessness. And we Christians can sometimes live with that kind of distorted theology when undergoing a period of trial and suffering. Our tendency then is not to view God as a loving heavenly Father who feels our pains and distresses, but as a cruel vindictive tyrant who takes advantage of our weakness like 'a giant torturing an insect'. But not only is it irreverent to allow our afflictions to lead us to think of God in this way, but it is counter-productive to our own

Chapter 6

peace of mind and heart and can plunge us into the depths of hopelessness and despair. God never belittles those whom he has made in his own image and likeness, and for whom he suffered himself in the sacrifice of his beloved Son. Indeed the very reverse is true. Someone else asked the same question as Job but came up with a very different answer: 'what is man that you are mindful of him, the son of man that you care for him? You made him a little lower than the heavenly beings and crowned him with glory and honour' (Psalm 8:4–5). The Psalmist is overwhelmed with the important place that man has in the vastness of God's creation, giving him the right to govern all things: 'You made him ruler over the works of your hands' (Psalm 8:6). Unlike Job, the Psalmist sees God's attention to man as elevating him, reminding him that he is different from the rest of creation because he is made in God's image, a living soul who can have a personal relationship with his Creator. God is indeed the 'watcher of men', as Job says, but not in order to harm us. Rather, it is because he is concerned about us and, in the Lord Jesus Christ, he has come so close to us as to enter into all our human experiences, even to the extent of bearing our sins in his own body on the cross.

Chapter 7

Bildad, an unsympathetic friend

Read Job chapter 8

In this chapter Bildad, another of Job's friends, enters the discussion. We get the feeling that he has listened quietly to the dialogue between Job and Eliphaz, but now he breaks abruptly into the argument, and we detect a certain impatience in his manner and a distinct lack of sympathy with Job's situation. 'Then Bildad the Shuhite replied: "How long will you say such things? Your words are a blustering wind"' (Job 8:1–2).

The power of words

Bildad comes on a bit strong with Job and accuses him of being no more than a 'windbag', mouthing meaningless and destructive words about God's injustice and lack of care. That is hardly a kind way to speak to someone whose heart is breaking. It is true that Job has said some very hard and irreverent things about God, but Bildad should have realised that here was a man speaking out of his brokenness, and then he might have been a little more tactful and sympathetic. Nevertheless, there is a great deal of truth in what he says. Words are powerful things and sometimes, like a 'blustering wind' they can be terribly destructive. Words also have the power to bless and inspire and bring comfort and hope. The Lord Jesus gave an ominous warning about the words we use: 'For out of the overflow of the heart the mouth speaks ... But I tell you that men will have to give account on the day of judgment for every careless word they have spoken. For by your words you will be acquitted, and by your words you will be condemned' (Matthew 12:34–37). That is a solemn warning and reminds us that a man's words can be an index to his character.

The power of words for good or evil can be illustrated in many ways. One has only to think of the stirring speeches of Winston Churchill during the Second World War and how they inspired and put heart into the nation in

From despair to hope **45**

Chapter 7

what were dark days. But equally powerful, in the cause of evil, were the speeches of Hitler that mesmerised the German people and led them to follow him in the path to national destruction. It is the failure to guard our words that can so often cause tension and friction in personal relationships. And even in the church fellowship we have those who do the devil's work by stirring up strife and dissension through malicious gossip, the tainted hint, the little innuendo and the half-truth, all of which releases a little drop of poison which works its way through the whole system.

But, above all, the significance of words is to be seen in the fact that one of the greatest titles given to our Lord was 'the Word'. 'In the beginning was the Word, and the Word was with God, and the Word was God. He was with God in the beginning' (John 1:1–2). We use words to communicate with others and to make known our thoughts and intentions. Christ is the great communicator, the One who reveals the mind and will and intention of God for mankind. Yes, words are powerful things, and James was so right to devote a whole passage in his epistle to the use of the tongue and the power of words (James 3).

Being judgmental

Bildad continues to upbraid Job in a very judgmental way. 'Does God pervert justice? Does the Almighty pervert what is right? When your children sinned against him, he gave them over to the penalty of their sin' (Job 8:3–4). He says to Job in effect, 'Do you think God was unjust in destroying your children? Wasn't it their own fault, because they sinned against him and therefore he brought judgement upon them?' Now that was a dreadful and cruel thing to say, and it must have hurt Job terribly. Furthermore, Bildad seems to have forgotten what he had said only a moment or two before about words being as destructive as a 'blustering wind'. For by his judgmental attitude he was certainly being destructive. The truth was that, as far as Job's children were concerned, we are not told anything about them being guilty of sin against God. Besides, their sins (if any) were covered by Job's intercessory sacrifices (Job 1:5).

We can all of us be very judgmental at times and accuse others of wrongdoing when we do not even know all the facts. There is a saying, 'To know is to understand.' When we know the full circumstances surrounding

Bildad, an unsympathetic friend

a person's actions and behaviour we are less likely to be judgmental and more inclined to try to understand why they did what they did. Our Lord warns us against judging others too hastily. 'Do not judge or you too will be judged, and with the measure you use, it will be measured to you' (Matthew 7:1–2). He then follows that up with the parable about removing a speck from our brother's eye whilst we have a plank in our own. This does not mean that all human judgement is wrong. We are passing judgement on things and people all the time. Life is impossible without doing that. But the Lord Jesus is warning us against censorious and hypocritical judgement, or judging others self-righteously as if we ourselves were perfect. In short, we are not to adopt the judgmental attitude that Bildad had towards Job. Above all, we must never pass final judgement upon anyone, however bad or sinful they are. God alone can do that.

The impermanence of worldly things

So convinced is he that Job is guilty of some great sin that Bildad urges Job to take God back into his life. 'But if you will look to God and plead with the Almighty, if you are pure and upright, even now he will rouse himself on your behalf and restore you to your rightful place. Your beginnings will seem humble, so prosperous will your future be' (Job 8:5–7). What he says is true, but what he does not realise is that Job has not left God out of his life in the first place. Nevertheless, he urges Job to look to the accumulated wisdom and experience of the past, to learn that the man who leaves God out of account in his life is heading for disaster. 'Ask the former generations and find out what their fathers learned, for we were born only yesterday and know nothing, and our days on earth are but a shadow. Will they not instruct you and tell you? Will they not bring forth words from their understanding?' (Job 8:9–10).

He then comes up with three word-pictures to illustrate the passing nature of the things of this life. He is implying that Job's mistake may have been to depend too much on the things he had surrounded himself with. First, 'Can papyrus grow tall where there is no marsh? Can reeds thrive without water? While still growing and uncut they wither more quickly than grass. Such is the destiny of all who forget God; so perishes the hope of the godless' (Job 8:11–13). That is certainly true of many others, if not of

From despair to hope **47**

Chapter 7

Job. As long as he has his material things, the worldly man is fine; but take them away and his life, like the reed, begins to wither and finally collapses, because these are the props that have held him up. Second, 'What he trusts in is fragile; what he relies on is a spider's web. He leans on his web, but it gives way; he clings to it, but it does not hold' (Job 8:14–15). A spider's web is beautiful to look at, but it is fragile and easily destroyed. Material things are fine, but they do not last for ever, and at the extremities of life they are of little help because they provide no inner strength. Third, the materialist 'is like a well-watered plant in the sunshine, spreading its shoots ... it entwines its roots around a pile of rocks and looks for a place among the stones. But when it is torn from its spot, that place disowns it and says, "I never saw you." Surely its life withers away, and from the soil other plants grow' (Job 8:16–19). A healthy plant is a joy to look at, but then someone comes along and tears it up by the roots and its beauty is gone. The materialist centres all his thoughts and energy on this life and this world, but it is ephemeral and passing. One day death will come, and he is suddenly torn away from it all, only to have to face the judgement of God.

God's care of his own

In contrast with the materialist he has been describing, Bildad ends with a picture of the man whose faith is firmly rooted in God and, without knowing it, he speaks prophetically where Job is concerned. 'Surely God does not reject a blameless man or strengthen the hands of evildoers. He will yet fill your mouth with laughter and your lips with shouts of joy. Your enemies will be clothed in shame, and the tents of the wicked will be no more' (Job 8:20–22). This in fact is what happened to Job, as we learn from the end of the book. God honoured his spiritual integrity. 'The Lord blessed the latter part of Job's life more than the first' (Job 42:12). God does indeed watch over his own, although circumstances at times may tempt us to think otherwise. That is why he is always worthy of our worship and praise, even when there is nothing special in our lives to praise him for. We praise him for what he is in himself as one who guards and keeps, who is active and purposeful, and who in Christ has called us into a living personal relationship with himself. He never abandons us, not even in the time of crisis. He is always 'nearer than hands or feet, closer than breathing'.

Bildad, an unsympathetic friend

In his speech to Job, Bildad has said some very positive and helpful things, but he has not met Job at his point of need. Locked as he is within his own orthodox theology, Bildad sees everything in terms of black and white. His argument is that God is just and righteous, and he levels at Job the rhetorical question, 'Does God pervert justice? Does the Almighty pervert what is right?' (Job 8:3). The answer clearly is no; therefore the trouble through which Job is passing must be God's retribution because of his sin. The only hope Bildad offers is for Job to admit he is an evildoer, for 'God does not reject a blameless man' (Job 8:20). In response to Job's confession 'He will yet fill your mouth with laughter and your lips with shouts of joy' (Job 8:21).

This is all good advice on the part of Bildad, except that it does not answer Job's problem. He knows in his heart that his suffering cannot be God's retribution for sin because he has not committed any such sin. So why is he suffering? That is what plagues him, and that is where he needed the help of his friends, but he was not getting it. Could this same charge be levelled at some of our preaching, perhaps? Are we answering questions no one is asking, and failing to direct our message to the perplexities and trials people are having to face in today's world? We must preach to people rather than at people. Medication, though good in itself, is of little use to the patient if it fails to address his problem.

Chapter 8

Man's need of righteousness

Read Job chapters 9 and 10

In these two chapters Job replies to Bildad by agreeing in the first instance with all that he has said about God's justice, and how he will not reject a man who is blameless of sin and wrongdoing. 'Then Job replied: "Indeed, I know that this is true. But how can a mortal be righteous before God?"' (Job 9:1–2). That is an important question, not only for Job, but for everyone.

Why righteousness?

But what makes this question about righteousness so important? For Job it was important because he was concerned to prove to God his own righteousness and innocence with regard to the particular sin for which his friends had said he was suffering God's judgement. But the problem for men in general is even greater. How can we ever hope to be righteous in God's sight when we are so sinful, and God himself is perfect in purity and holiness? John Bradford, the English reformer and martyr (1510–1555), looking one day at a man going to the scaffold, said: 'But for the grace of God there goes John Bradford.' He was absolutely right. He knew well enough that in the depths of his own being he, and all of us, have the same dark powers and propensities that led that man to commit murder. That is what the Bible teaches: 'for all have sinned and fall short of the glory of God' (Romans 3:23). To be righteous before God means to be right with God, to be reconciled and at peace with God, to know that although you are not sinless, nevertheless God accepts you as if you were, and therefore your conscience no longer accuses you in the light of God's holiness. But how do we obtain this state of 'rightness' in our present sinful condition? Well, there are those who have their own ways of going about it.

Some think they can get right with God by comparing themselves with others. They look at the sins of other people, worse than themselves, and they think, 'Well, I'm not nearly so bad as that', and they derive a false sense of peace and comfort from thinking that they must therefore be acceptable

Man's need of righteousness

in God's sight. But that is a false comparison. Our Lord told a parable to warn us about that very danger:

To some who were confident of their own righteousness and looked down on everybody else, Jesus told this parable. Two men went up to the temple to pray, one a Pharisee and the other a tax collector. The Pharisee prayed about himself: 'God, I thank you that I am not like other men—robbers, evildoers, adulterers—or even like this tax collector. I fast twice a week and give a tenth of all I get.' But the tax collector ... would not even look up to heaven, but beat his breast and said, 'God, have mercy on me, a sinner.' I tell you that this man, rather than the other, went home justified before God (Luke 18:9–14).

Clearly, the only standard to compare ourselves with is the holiness of God himself, and we all fail there.

Some think they can get right with God by sentimentalising about his love and mercy. They say in effect, 'I know I am not all that I should be, and I break God's laws and commandments. But God, after all, is merciful and loving, and I feel certain that everything will work out in the end.' But to think like that is to be self-deluded. The Bible is absolutely clear: 'without holiness no-one will see the Lord' (Hebrews 12:14). We must never sentimentalise about sin, persuading ourselves that God can overlook it. He cannot. To do so would be untrue to his own nature. His justice demands that sin be punished.

Some think they can provide their own righteousness by striving sincerely to be so good and honest in God's sight that he will say at the judgement, 'Well done, you've made it at last. You've worked really hard at being righteous, and worthy enough to enter heaven and merit eternal life, and it's all yours.' But is that true? Can we ever make ourselves good enough and pure enough to satisfy the holiness of God and to live in his presence? According to the Bible, even our goodness is tainted with sin: 'all our righteous acts are like filthy rags' (Isaiah 64:6).

The greatness of God

Aware as he is of his own weakness and imperfection, Job continues to reflect on God's greatness. 'Though one wished to dispute with him, he

Chapter 8

could not answer him one time out of a thousand. His wisdom is profound, his power is vast. Who has resisted him and come out unscathed?' (Job 9:3–4). The picture he has in mind is that of a courtroom scene: God is the judge, and man is standing before him trying to prove his righteousness. But it is hopeless, for God can bring a thousand charges against sinful man and he would not be able to refute one of them. God could say to any one of us: 'So you think you are worthy and righteous enough to merit heaven and eternal life? Very well, let me test you. Have you never been unselfish and unkind? Never lied or been angry? Never allowed lust and greed to dominate you? Never suffered from pride or had evil thoughts?' So the charges would mount up, and we would not be able to refute them. For the truth is that in the greatness of his power God sees us not as we would like him to see us, but as we really are. Others might say of us, 'What a wonderful person! A true saint, if ever there was one! If anyone deserves to go to heaven, he (or she) does.' But they do not know the real you or me. Only God has the greatness and power and wisdom to know us as we really are, because he created us.

Then, in the following verses, Job gives a magnificent poetic description of God's might and majesty. 'He moves mountains without their knowing it and overturns them in his anger. He shakes the earth from its place and makes its pillars tremble. He speaks to the sun and it does not shine; he seals off the light of the stars. He alone stretches out the heavens and treads on the waves of the sea. He is the maker of the Bear and Orion, the Pleiades and the constellations of the south. He performs wonders that cannot be fathomed, miracles that cannot be numbered' (Job 9:5–10). Faced with the immensity of such a God, how can man ever hope to dispute with him on equal terms? 'How then can I dispute with him? How can I find words to argue with him?' (Job 9:14). Job continues in this vein down to verse 31, and then he ends the picture of the courtroom scene with an appeal for someone to arbitrate or mediate between himself and this mighty majestic God.

Our need of a mediator

'He is not a man like me that I might answer him, that we might confront each other in court. If only there were someone to arbitrate between us, to lay his hand upon us both, someone to remove God's rod from me, so that

Man's need of righteousness

his terror would frighten me no more. Then I would speak up without fear of him, but as it now stands with me, I cannot' (Job 9:32–35). He may not have realised the full prophetic import of what he was saying, but in answer to the original question 'How can a mortal be righteous before God?' he is pointing us in the right direction by expressing the need for an arbiter or mediator to plead our cause. Who is there who can remove 'God's rod' of judgement upon our sin? Who is there who is human enough to identify with our fallen sinful nature on the one hand, and yet on the other hand holy and pure enough to plead our cause with God on equal terms?

The New Testament answer to that is unequivocal: 'For there is one God and one mediator between God and men, the man Christ Jesus, who gave himself as a ransom for all men' (1 Timothy 2:5). As our mediator Christ interposed himself between the 'offended God' and the 'offending sinner', taking upon himself 'God's rod' of judgement upon man's sin. He did this through his sacrifice on the cross, thus becoming 'our righteousness, holiness and redemption' (1 Corinthians 1:30).

No easy solutions

As we move into chapter 10 we find Job once more falling into the rebellious and bitter mood that we encountered back in chapter 3. The dark images of death and the grave once again seem to dominate his thinking. 'I loathe my very life; therefore I will give free rein to my complaint and speak out in the bitterness of my soul' (Job 10:1). And again, 'Why then did you bring me out of the womb? I wish I had died before any eye saw me. If only I had never come into being, or had been carried straight from the womb to the grave! Are not my few days almost over? Turn away from me so that I can have a moment's joy before I go to the place of no return, to the land of gloom and deep shadow, to the land of deepest night, of deep shadow and disorder, where even the light is like darkness' (Job 10:18–22). It is all very depressing and, as one commentator says, it serves as 'a reminder that the sickroom is not the place to argue theology'.

In his perplexity and bewilderment at what is happening to him, Job bombards God with a whole number of questions to which he would like answers. 'I will say to God: Do not condemn me, but tell me what charges you have against me. Does it please you to oppress me, to spurn the work of

Chapter 8

your hands, while you smile on the schemes of the wicked? Do you have eyes of flesh? Do you see as a mortal sees? Are your days like those of a mortal or your years like those of a man, that you must search out my faults and probe after my sin—though you know that I am not guilty and that no-one can rescue me from your hand?' (Job 10:2–7). What all this is saying to us is that there are no easy solutions to the problems we encounter as God's children, neither are there any easy answers to some of the questions that arise in our minds concerning God's dealings with us.

There is a mysterious side to God's being with which, somehow or other, we cannot get to grips. Among the last words of Moses to the children of Israel was the reminder that 'The secret things belong to the Lord our God' (Deuteronomy 29:9). There are indeed many such secret things and, as happened with Job, they can create in us a lot of frustration at the intellectual level, and a good deal of anguish at the emotional and spiritual level. In a certain sense, therefore, I suppose it is easier to be an atheist in this life than it is to be a Christian. The atheist, after all, has no sense of accountability to God for his actions, and he is certainly not plagued with the dilemma of trying to reconcile God's love for him in the Lord Jesus Christ with the feeling, at certain times in his life, that God seems unloving and uncaring. This of course is one of the main themes of the book of Job, and we shall have to come back to it again in greater detail in chapter 23, where he cries from the heart, 'If only I knew where to find him' (verse 3). But, for the time being, let us keep in mind that the main purpose of the gospel is not to make us happy, or to provide a featherbed existence and a life free from difficult and awkward questions. Its main purpose is to reconcile us to God in Christ, and in furtherance of that we are promised the Holy Spirit to help us in our weakness—and that includes our intellectual weakness (Romans 8:26–27). When we look at what lies ahead for the Christian, therefore, it is surely the case that no suffering in this life, physical, emotional or intellectual, is 'worth comparing with the glory that will be revealed in us'.

God's creative act

In a powerful passage, full of poetic imagery, Job touches upon the important subject of God's creative act in conception and birth. 'Your hands shaped me and made me. Will you now turn and destroy me? Remember that you moulded me like clay. Will you now turn me to dust again? Did you not pour me out like milk and curdle me like cheese, clothe me with skin and flesh and knit me together with bones and sinews? You gave me life and showed me kindness, and in your providence watched over my spirit' (Job 10:8–12). In spite of all his complaining and bitterness, it is inconceivable to Job's mind that the God who had so wonderfully created him in the womb should now want to destroy his own handiwork. The expression about curdling milk into cheese is a reference to the mysterious act of conception, and is in keeping with other passages in the Bible which speak of life beginning at this point. The Psalmist says, 'I praise you because I am fearfully and wonderfully made; your works are wonderful, I know that full well. My frame was not hidden from you when I was made in the secret place. When I was woven together in the depths of the earth, your eyes saw my unformed body' (Psalm 139:14–16). And we read in Jeremiah, 'Before I formed you in the womb I knew you, before you were born I set you apart' (Jeremiah 1:5).

All this is far removed from the language of today's abortionist, who speaks of the embryo as a 'product' of conception, or 'womb tissue', or 'a collection of cells'. It reminds us that we each have our own special personality and identity as God's handiwork, and that we are not merely an evolutionary product that survives for a little while, and then decays and falls to the ground like a leaf on a tree. Rather, we are created in God's own image and likeness (Genesis 1:26), and we have an immortal soul and spirit, which he desires to nourish in order to bring out our full potential for his glory and to fulfil his purpose in the world.

But Job's profound conviction that it was God who created him in the womb only serves to increase his perplexity concerning God's purpose in allowing him to be born in the first instance, when he faced only suffering and trial in this life. 'Why then did you bring me out of the womb?' (Job 10:18). It is this resounding Why? that always confronts us in the face of life's sufferings. Where is the sense of it all? Why have a life in the first place, if it only means spending one's days in a wheelchair or in a mental hospital? There are no easy answers to these questions, not even in the book of Job, which was written to give us insights into the dilemmas presented by the

Chapter 8

world's suffering. But the Bible, including the book of Job, affirms positively that God is a God of love. That being so, our faith must be able to hold in tension both the fact of God's goodness and the fact of sin with its attendant suffering. There are dreadful evils in the world, but that is not the whole story. There is also much that is good and beautiful and that enriches our lives, such as the love of family and friends, the delights of nature, the pleasures associated with art and literature. But the main reason the Christian is able to live with the question Why? is because he knows that God has proved his love for us in his own suffering, in the sacrifice of his Son on the cross for our salvation.

Chapter 9

Godliness without winsomeness

Read Job chapter 11

In this chapter Zophar, the third of Job's friends, makes his contribution to the discussion. Like Eliphaz and Bildad, he too is convinced in his own mind that Job has committed some great sin against God, and that this accounts for the suffering he is enduring. He begins by being extremely hard and critical towards Job. 'Then Zophar the Naamathite replied: "Are all these words to go unanswered? Is this talker to be vindicated? Will your idle talk reduce men to silence? Will no-one rebuke you when you mock? You say to God, 'My beliefs are flawless and I am pure in your sight.' Oh, how I wish that God would speak, that he would open his lips against you and disclose to you the secrets of wisdom, for true wisdom has two sides. Know this: God has even forgotten some of your sin"' (Job 11:1–6).

Good but hard

We cannot doubt that Zophar, like the other friends, was a good and godly man. But it is evident from his strong attack upon Job that he lacked compassion and that there was a certain hardness in his godliness. He condemns Job out of hand and brings a string of accusations against him of the most vicious kind. He says that Job is insincere, a man who is full of sanctimonious talk, but whose words are not backed up with a holy life. He accuses him of mocking God and claiming to be 'flawless' and 'pure' in God's sight. But none of these things was actually true of Job. Certainly he had said some very irreverent things about God, but he had never mocked him, neither had he ever claimed sinless perfection.

We can sometimes be too critical of others, can't we? As we said, Zophar was a godly man, but he reminds us of those Christians who have a hard, critical streak running through their spirituality, which makes it unattractive to others and, instead of drawing them to Christ, only succeeds in repelling

From despair to hope 57

Chapter 9

them. This was one of the essential differences between the Lord Jesus and the scribes and Pharisees. Again and again we read in the Gospels of the compassion and tenderness of Jesus in dealing with people. 'When Jesus landed and saw a large crowd, he had compassion on them, because they were like sheep without a shepherd. So he began teaching them many things' (Mark 6:34). His heart went out to them because he saw them as people who were lost and bewildered, without direction and guidance in life. This did not mean that, in teaching them, he failed to talk firmly about sin and the need for repentance and faith, but he did it with love and winsomeness. The religious leaders on the other hand, although they were good men and pillars of orthodoxy, had a harshness about them that made their talk of God and religion sound hard and uninviting.

There were those, of course, who rejected Christ in spite of his winsomeness, but that was because they could not accept the truth of which he spoke, and not because of the manner in which he said it.

Forgiving and forgetting

But what Zophar said to Job was not all negative. He had some positive things to say as well. 'Know this: God has even forgotten some of your sin' (Job 11:6). Or, to put it another way, 'God has not judged you to the full extent of your sin.' Or again, 'God has not punished you to the degree your sins deserve.' This is an echo of the Psalmist's words: 'he does not treat us as our sins deserve, or repay us according to our iniquities' (Psalm 103:10). And that is certainly true. God does not judge us according to our sin but according to his grace. If this were not true we should have no hope of salvation. Furthermore, in the sacrifice of Christ it is not only 'some' of our sin, as Zophar says, that God has forgiven and forgotten, but the whole of our sin. As the hymn says:

> My sin—O the bliss of this glorious thought!—
> My sin, not in part, but the whole,
> Is nailed to His cross, and I bear it no more:
> Praise the Lord, praise the Lord, O my soul!

Jeremiah anticipates the new covenant in Christ when he says to the people on God's behalf: 'For I will forgive their wickedness and will remember their sins no more' (Jeremiah 31:34). Some Christians find it hard to believe that God not only forgave them their sins when they came to faith in Christ, but that he forgot them as well, buried them, removed them 'as far as the east is from the west'. The result is that their Christian vitality is sapped by the constant sense of failure and defeat over past sins. I remember reading somewhere about tribal hostility in Polynesia, where each family would keep a reminder of their hatred in the form of an article or piece of clothing suspended from the roof of their hut so as to keep alive the memory of past wrongs done to them. If we have really repented of past sins, we must never allow the painful memory of them to vitiate our spiritual strength and prevent us from going forward in the Christian life. God says that he has forgotten them, and so should we.

Can we know God?

Zophar raises another important subject in the form of a question and answer in his interrogation of Job. 'Can you fathom the mysteries of God? Can you probe the limits of the Almighty? They are higher than the heavens—what can you do? They are deeper than the depths of the grave—what can you know? Their measure is longer than the earth and wider than the sea ... But a witless man can no more become wise than a wild donkey's colt can be born a man' (Job 11:7–12). He is saying that God is so different from ourselves, so transcendent in his being, that a man has about as much hope of becoming wise enough to know him and to understand the complexities of his ways as a donkey has of becoming a man. And he is right. Man by his own power can never get to know God, let alone understand him.

One of the most important questions to face man is this: If there is such a thing as ultimate truth, how can one lay hold of it? The history of religion is man's attempt to answer that question. Some will claim that we can know ultimate truth through meditation, or through mysticism or ritual or philosophy. But man by his own unaided efforts can never come to this ultimate knowledge of God, as Zophar says, because God is eternal and infinite and man is temporal and finite. The only hope for man, therefore, would be for God to make himself known to him. And that is what he has

Chapter 9

done in the revelation he has given in creation (Romans 1:19–20), in the Bible (2 Peter 1:20–21), and finally in the person of his Son, the Lord Jesus Christ (Hebrews 1:1–3).

Returning to God

In his closing words to Job Zophar assures him that however great his guilt, and however far he has strayed from God, there is always a way back.

Yet if you devote your heart to him and stretch out your hands to him, if you put away the sin that is in your hand and allow no evil to dwell in your tent, then you will lift up your face without shame; you will stand firm and without fear. You will surely forget your trouble, recalling it only as waters gone by. Life will be brighter than noonday, and darkness will become like morning. You will be secure, because there is hope; you will look about you and take your rest in safety. You will lie down, with no-one to make you afraid, and many will court your favour (Job 11:13–19).

That is a very positive and encouraging word. Although Zophar is mistaken in thinking that Job is guilty, the principle he enunciates is nevertheless right.

When he urges Job to 'stretch out [his] hands to him', he is saying that the way back to restored fellowship with God when we have strayed from him is through humble repentance. Sin and disobedience bring judgement, but repentance and obedience bring blessing. When we wander from God, our Christian life becomes dry and unsatisfying and loses the glow we once knew in his service. But it does not have to remain like that. We can get out of the hole we have dug for ourselves if we have the will to do it. The prodigal in the far country said to himself, 'I will set out and go back to my father' (Luke 15:18). To return to the father was a deliberate act of will on his part. '"Return to me," declares the Lord Almighty, "and I will return to you"' (Zechariah 1:3).

A word of warning

Zophar's final word is one of grave warning to anyone who thinks he can trifle with God. 'But the eyes of the wicked will fail, and escape will elude them; their hope will become a dying gasp.' In the light of what has been said about knowing God, and receiving his forgiveness through repentance and faith, a man may still not wish to do any of these things. He may continue to spurn God, and delight in continuing his own chosen and sinful way. But if he does so, then his life will end in miserable failure—a lost soul separated from God for ever. With such folk in mind Zophar uses the phrase 'and escape will elude them'. He means that for such a person there is no escape from the wrath and judgement of God at the end of this life. And that is also the clear teaching of the gospel: 'how shall we escape if we ignore such a great salvation?' (Hebrews 2:3).

Chapter 10

Human arrogance

Read Job chapter 12

In this and the following two chapters (13 and 14) Job replies to the arguments and criticisms of all three friends. Although each was different in temperament and manner, all three were agreed that Job was guilty before God and deserved the punishment which, they believed, he was receiving. It was this arrogant assumption of guilt, and their tone of superiority, that Job found so irksome and irritating, and that leads him to speak his mind and tell them a few home truths that they needed to hear.

No one is indispensable

He begins his reply with biting sarcasm. 'Then Job replied: "Doubtless you are the people, and wisdom will die with you! But I have a mind as well as you; I am not inferior to you. Who does not know all these things?"' (Job 12:1–3). He seems to be saying, 'How arrogant and conceited can you get? You think that when you die, all wisdom and knowledge will come to an end, and the human race will be so impoverished without you that it will never recover. Remember this, your advice and wisdom is not indispensable, and therefore you shouldn't talk down to me as though I were some kind of inferior being.' We sense how very angry and upset he is. From their self-opinionated pinnacle they were looking down on him, and arrogantly criticising his lack of spirituality and failure to understand God, when he knows in his heart that he is innocent of any wrongdoing, and has always been faithful in serving God.

Human pride and arrogance are always hard to stomach, but especially when they spring from a sense of spiritual superiority. For there are folk like that, including pastors, who think that unless they are always there propping up God's work, giving advice and pontificating on every issue, then the cause of God will collapse. That is why some pastors find it difficult to delegate responsibility to others. They think they are indispensable. What conceited nonsense that is! No one is indispensable in God's cause. Peter and Paul, the Church Fathers, Luther and Calvin, Wesley and Whitefield, Spurgeon and Moody—all these men did their work and left this world, but the cause of God goes on. 'God buries his workmen but carries on his work.' He carries it on because the work of the gospel is far bigger than any of us. God in his mercy and grace chooses to use us in his work, but he never has to depend on us. That is a humbling thought for some of us, but it helps us to keep our place in God's scheme of things in true perspective. 'God opposes the proud but gives grace to the humble' (1 Peter 5:5).

This thought of human arrogance has a much wider application when we think of today's world. Modern man, in his intellectual conceit and arrogance, has no need of God, no need of forgiveness and no sense of dependence on any higher power. 'What do we need God for?' he says in effect. 'Our forefathers in their ignorance may have needed that kind of naive belief, but we have no need of it today. We have progressed far beyond that kind of simplistic thinking. We must believe in ourselves, in our own capacities and abilities, our own intellectual powers to unravel the mysteries of life and of the universe. We have no need any longer to be dependent on the notion of some benevolent father-god figure.' This may all sound plausible enough—until you take a realistic look at the kind of world this arrogant, self-assertive attitude has produced.

Ours is a world full of wretchedness, greed and violence. It is a world which, on its own admission, is in danger of obliterating itself through the destruction of its own life-giving resources. We have polluted the oceans, destroyed the forests, decimated the wildlife, created vast dust bowls where nothing grows, and poisoned the very air we breathe. I heard on a television programme recently that through neglect and pollution we have so reduced our fresh-water resources that, if we carry on in the same way, we can anticipate the possibility of 'water wars' in the future, as nations fight to keep control of this precious resource. So much then for man's arrogant claim to be self-sufficient and independent. It is only when he is willing to come down from this self-opinionated pinnacle of pride in his own achievements, and turn to God with a sense of humble need, that there is any hope of man's own salvation and that of his world.

Chapter 10

Contempt for others

Job continues to reproach his friends for their treatment of him. 'I have become a laughing-stock to my friends, though I called upon God and he answered—a mere laughing-stock, though righteous and blameless! Men at ease have contempt for misfortune as the fate of those whose feet are slipping. The tents of marauders are undisturbed, and those who provoke God are secure—those who carry their god in their hands' (Job 12:4–6). He feels that his friends, by their unjust criticism of him and by their unkind words, have made him an object of contempt and derision, despite the fact that in happier days he had prayed to God and received answers to his prayers. What was particularly cruel, to his mind, was that his friends were speaking in this contemptuous manner from their own position of security and plenty, whereas he was on his beam-ends, having lost everything, his family and livelihood. With all their talk about God's justice and righteous living, what they were really doing was preaching at him instead of to him. Or, as we might say today, they were 'kicking a man when he was down'. What Job needed in his situation was not criticism and profound talk about God and righteousness, but a practical expression of godly help and comfort. The talk could come later.

There are times in the Christian life, and in our relations with others, when words can never be a substitute for action, and to make them so is to show a contempt for the humanity of others. James had this in mind when he says: 'What good is it, my brothers, if a man claims to have faith but has no deeds? Can such faith save him? Suppose a brother or sister is without clothes and daily food. If one of you says to him, "Go, I wish you well; keep warm and well fed," but does nothing about his physical needs, what good is it? In the same way, faith by itself, if it is not accompanied by action, is dead' (James 2:14–17). We might call this the performance gap—the difference between what we say about the gospel and the way we live it out in practice. If a person is in need of physical and material help, and we are content to give him the gospel in words without translating it into direct action, we are showing contempt for his God-given humanity.

But it goes even further than that. Today in our society people are conditioned by performance: it underlies everything, sport, politics and commercial life. The television adverts show the extraordinary length and expense to which big business will go in order to impress upon us that their product tastes better, or goes faster, or washes whiter, etc. The whole psychology is based on the idea that performance proves the value of the product. And people often judge the gospel in the same way. They watch us as believers to see if our performance verifies the product, that is, the Christian message. And if it does not, then no matter how eloquent or forceful we are in presenting that message, in their eyes the gospel will have failed and is brought into contempt.

God's sovereign power

In the final section of this chapter (verses 7–25) Job eloquently expounds God's providential government of the world. He wants his friends to know that, despite the harsh things he has said about God, deep down in his heart he really does believe that God is controlling all things by his wisdom and power. God does what he pleases in creation and in the affairs of men— including his own suffering—and we just have to accept that fact. He begins with God's rule in creation:

But ask the animals, and they will teach you, or the birds of the air, and they will tell you; or speak to the earth, and it will teach you, or let the fish of the sea inform you. Which of all these does not know that the hand of the Lord has done this? In his hand is the life of every creature and the breath of all mankind. Does not the ear test words as the tongue tastes food? Is not wisdom found among the aged? Does not long life bring understanding? To God belong wisdom and power; counsel and understanding are his. What he tears down cannot be rebuilt; the man he imprisons cannot be released. If he holds back the waters, there is drought; if he lets them loose, they devastate the land (Job 12:7–15).

If we unpack this, we find that what Job is saying is that creation itself testifies to God's providential government. Man likes to think that he controls his natural environment and that he can do what he likes with it; hence the many serious ecological problems facing us today. But, as if to show man who is really in charge, God every so often lets loose his destructive power in nature. 'If he holds back the waters, there is drought; if he lets them loose they devastate the land.' That is so true! At the moment

Chapter 10

of writing, many countries in Europe, including Hungary, Poland and East Germany, are experiencing the worst floods in living memory, with thousands being made homeless, and all our cleverness and technology can do nothing about it.

In the light of that we can see what Job means when he says: 'Does not the ear test words as the tongue tastes food?' Just as our palate discriminates by taste between one kind of food and another, so our minds should discriminate between truth and error in what is said, written and preached concerning God and his ways. Such discernment is greatly needed in the Church today and it is the Holy Spirit who imparts it to us. Going a step further, Job speaks of God's control over man's history. 'To him belong strength and victory; both deceived and deceiver are his. He leads counsellors away stripped and makes fools of judges. He takes off the shackles put on by kings and ties a loincloth round their waist. He leads priests away stripped and overthrows men long established ... He makes nations great, and destroys them; he enlarges nations, and disperses them' (Job 12:16–23).

One of the most significant shifts that has taken place in today's thinking is the denial that there is such a thing as the power of God. Modern man suffers from a power complex. In a sense he has always had it since Satan appealed to it when he said to our first parents: 'For God knows that when you eat of it your eyes will be opened, and you will be like God, knowing good and evil' (Genesis 3:5). And that has been man's trouble ever since. He believes he has the godlike power to control his own destiny and that of his world. He fails to understand that ultimately all power belongs to God. That is what Job had in mind when he says, 'He deprives the leaders of the earth of their reason; he sends them wandering through a trackless waste. They grope in darkness with no light; he makes them stagger like drunkards' (Job 12:24–25). The leaders and governments of the world, if they continue to rely solely upon the exercise of their own political, economic and military power rather than upon God's power, will inevitably lead mankind into a 'trackless waste' and plunge our world into final darkness.

It is worth reminding ourselves that when Pilate, the representative of the greatest power on earth at that time, said to Jesus, 'Don't you realise I have power either to free you or to crucify you?' our Lord replied, 'You would have no power over me if it were not given to you from above' (John 19:10–11). That is echoing Job's assertion—all power belongs to God.

Chapter 11

Talking things through with God

Read Job chapter 13

Job continues to reply to the criticisms and arguments of his friends Eliphaz, Bildad and Zophar, and he begins by reasserting what he had said in the previous chapter about his absolute confidence in the sovereignty of God's wisdom and power in the affairs of men and nations. 'My eyes have seen all this, my ears have heard and understood it. What you know, I also know; I am not inferior to you' (Job 13:1–2). He affirms his own personal knowledge and experience of God. He is saying to his friends, 'You may have your own theories about God and his ways with men, but I can assure you I too have my own experience of God working in my life. So don't talk down to me as though I were inferior to you in all this.' And of course he was absolutely right. We all have our own personal experience of God, and that is what really matters. It is not enough to have a head knowledge of God and to theorise about his ways, which is what characterised much of the advice of Job's friends. We need to know God at the level of our own personal experience of his love to us in the Lord Jesus Christ. This close intimate relationship with God is the theme of this chapter and Job leads in to it with what is the key verse: 'But I desire to speak to the Almighty and to argue my cause with God' (Job 13:3).

Getting close to God

He is saying to his friends, 'I've listened to you long enough, and your advice has not helped me one bit. So I am now going to talk things through with God.' Then, in sheer exasperation, he describes in very harsh terms how useless they had been. 'You, however, smear me with lies; you are worthless physicians, all of you! If only you would be altogether silent! For you, that would be wisdom. Hear now my argument; listen to the plea of my lips' (Job 13:4–6). He even accuses them of doing God a grave disservice by trying to present his case for him. 'Will you speak wickedly on God's behalf? Will you speak deceitfully for him? Will you show him partiality? Will you argue the case for God?' (Job 13:7–8).

What we learn from all this is that there are times in life when we have to go beyond what man can do for us or say to us, and get close enough to God to talk things through with him. It is good and helpful to have friends to talk to when we are in trouble, although sometimes, like Job's friends, they can make matters worse. But even when their advice and comfort are helpful and encouraging, they cannot always enter fully into our situation because their knowledge and ability are limited. Or it may be that at the practical level there is nothing they can do. How often have we ourselves said about a situation in which we have wanted to be of help, 'If only there were something I could do!' Henry Francis Lyte puts it so well in his magnificent hymn 'Abide with me':

> When other helpers fail, and comforts flee,
> Help of the helpless, O abide with me.

This business of going beyond men and getting close to God to talk things through with him is what we mean by prayer. Prayer ought never to be an irksome duty, something we are reluctant to start and glad to finish, but an exercise we derive pleasure from because it is 'the Christian's vital breath' and his 'native air'. Job says what he wants is to 'speak to the Almighty' so that he might argue his case with him. And that is a legitimate element in prayer—talking things through, laying things out before him, arguing or reasoning with him, not in a spirit of rebellion but in a spirit of reverence and simple trust. God himself urges us to that: '"Come now, let us reason together," says the Lord' (Isaiah 1:18).

But in order to feel free to talk things through with God, and to reason or argue our case with him, we must first be close to him. It is only with a close friend that we are able to discuss intimate things, not with a nodding acquaintance. Our longing for God needs to be much stronger than it is. The Psalmist cried, 'O God, you are my God, earnestly I seek you; my soul thirsts for you, my body longs for you, in a dry and weary land where there is no water' (Psalm 63:1). When our desire for God reaches that intensity,

Chapter 11

prayer, or talking things through with him, becomes the most natural thing in the world. We will feel the 'need to tell him of our desires and disappointments, our doubts and our strivings. We need to be quiet, to listen, to wait. We need to be with him in our sinfulness and forgiveness. We need to let him know who we are and how we are, to let him be our strength in our weakness. We need to let him be the God he wants to be through us' (*Still Waters, Deep Waters* by Rowland Croucher, page 45).

Deception

But in this matter of getting close to God we have to be careful that we do not deceive ourselves and others. Job warns his friends that they may be guilty of just that. 'Would it turn out well if he examined you? Could you deceive him as you might deceive men? He would surely rebuke you if you secretly showed partiality. Would not his splendour terrify you? Would not the dread of him fall on you? Your maxims are proverbs of ashes; your defences are defences of clay' (Job 13:9–12). He is saying to them, 'You've talked a good deal about God's righteousness and justice, but what would happen, I wonder, if he were to examine your faith and put it to the test in the way he is testing my faith at the moment? Your fine words and profession of faith may sound well in the ears of men; you may deceive them, and you may even deceive yourselves; but you don't deceive God. Under the scrutiny and examination of his searching truth your fine maxims and wise sayings are as worthless as ashes, and in the face of trial and suffering your faith in God would collapse like a house of clay.'

Could that be true of us? Are we deceiving others and ourselves as to the reality of our Christian faith? Does our closeness to God go no deeper, in the last analysis, than the testimony of our words? In his novel *The Brothers Karamazov*, Dostoyevsky has the story of an elderly doctor who talked a lot about loving humanity, and genuinely believed he did. But when he had to spend twenty-four hours in the same room as a man with a heavy cold who was constantly blowing his nose, he was horrified to discover that he was actually beginning to hate the man and was glad to get away from him. That simple test proved the vanity and emptiness of all his talk about loving humanity, and showed him that he was self-deceived. Perhaps it would turn out like that with us, if God were to examine the reality of our love for him tomorrow by putting our faith to the test in the face of some great trial. We should suddenly find, to our shock and horror, that our love is as worthless as ashes and that our faith begins to crack and crumble like a house of clay.

This whole question of deception in relation to the Christian life, whether it is deceiving ourselves or deceiving others, is a very solemn one, and our Lord himself deals with it in a manner that reveals its frightening implications. 'Not everyone who says to me, "Lord, Lord" will enter the kingdom of heaven, but only he who does the will of my Father who is in heaven. Many will say to me on that day, "Lord, Lord, did we not prophesy in your name, and in your name drive out demons and perform many miracles?" Then I will tell them plainly, "I never knew you. Away from me, you evildoers"' (Matthew 7:21–23). That is a truly frightening statement. For here were people who were saying the right things ("Lord, Lord"), and doing the right things in prophesying and performing miracles; and yet the Lord says they did not belong to him. They were deceiving themselves and others, in thinking they were Christians when in fact they were not. They had depended for their salvation on their profession of faith in Christ, calling him "Lord, Lord", but they had not shown the reality of that faith in the life they had lived. In the words of Jesus, they had not done 'the will of my Father in heaven'.

A man can do the right thing from the wrong motive—even prophesying and performing miracles. Jesus condemned these people as 'evildoers', not because of their preaching and miracle working but because they were not right with God in their hearts. They professed him as Lord, but were not united with him inwardly, therefore he says to them, 'I never knew you.' They had deceived themselves and others, but they could not deceive God. This can only mean that whatever power they had exercised was not of God but of the devil. Satan had manipulated them, for he is the arch-deceiver who masquerades, when it suits him, as an angel of light. Our closeness to God, therefore, must go a lot deeper than an outward profession of faith, or having the right theology, or doing the right things in the eyes of others. We must know the saving grace of Christ in our heart and have the seed of new life inwardly planted by the Holy Spirit.

Chapter 11

Confidence and doubt

One very significant feature in Job's relationship with God is the way he oscillates between confidence and doubt. This comes out very strongly in the closing verses of this chapter when he turns from his friends and addresses God.

Keep silent and let me speak; then let come to me what may. Why do I put myself in jeopardy and take my life in my hands? Though he slay me, yet will I hope in him; I will surely defend my ways to his face. Indeed, this will turn out for my deliverance, for no godless man would dare come before him! Listen carefully to my words; let your ears take in what I say. Now that I have prepared my case, I know I will be vindicated. Can anyone bring charges against me? If so, I will be silent and die (Job 13:13–19).

We detect a strong note of confidence in his words as he prepares to address God. Whatever his friends may think, he is certain that God knows the true state of his heart, and that he will be vindicated. He is not even afraid to die and meet with God, for he is confident of his salvation: 'Though he slay me, yet will I hope in him.'

At the same time he still has many doubts and questions in his mind, as the following verses show. 'Only grant me these two things, O God, and then I will not hide from you: Withdraw your hand far from me, and stop frightening me with your terrors' (Job 13:20–21). He is terrified by the thought that God's hand of judgement is upon him. 'Why do you hide your face and consider me your enemy? Will you torment a wind-blown leaf? Will you chase after dry chaff?' (Job 13:24–25). He wonders why God has removed his blessing from him, and continually harasses and torments him. 'You fasten my feet in shackles; you keep close watch on all my paths by putting marks on the soles of my feet' (Job 13:27). He feels he is a slave or prisoner who has been branded to prevent him escaping. Although he clings tenaciously to his hope in God, it is evident that Job's confidence has taken a severe battering as a result of what has happened to him.

Confidence and doubt are two sides of the religious experience which people have always wrestled with, and never more so than at the present time. We are living in an age of doubt, and ours is a society in which every cherished belief is challenged and nothing is sacred. Young people in our schools and universities are encouraged to doubt and question every aspect of religious truth and to take nothing for granted. This is especially true of Christianity. The being of God, the divinity of Christ, the Bible, the Church and miracles are all critically examined. But much of this, rather than being honest doubt which seeks only the truth, is deliberate scepticism and rank unbelief, with a lot of pride attaching to it, and is so typical of man's wisdom, which refuses to accept what it does not understand. And we have to be careful that we do not allow Satan to exploit our doubts in this way and turn them into unbelief. As long as we are in this sinful world, the believer will always have this struggle between confidence and doubt, hope and fear, trust and despair, since it is a part of the spiritual warfare he is engaged in as a child of God. The important thing is that we do not struggle with our doubts on our own. We must seek God's help by acting on the faith we have. Nowhere is this more clearly seen in the New Testament than in the case of the father of the boy healed of an evil spirit. In response to our Lord's assurance, 'Everything is possible for him who believes', the father cried, 'I do believe; help me overcome my unbelief!' (Mark 9:23–24). In spite of our lingering unbelief God does help us, so that feeble faith becomes strong, and doubt turns to confidence.

Chapter 12

The brevity of life

Read Job chapter 14

The pessimism and doubt concerning God's ways which had plagued Job's mind at the close of the previous chapter still dominates his thinking in chapter 14, as he continues to reject the argument of his friends that his suffering is related to sin and retribution, and as he reflects on the brevity and fragility of man's life in this world. 'Man born of woman is of few days and full of trouble' (Job 14:1). On the face of it, it seems a dark and dismal chapter, and so it is. But at one point Job's spirit soars above his 'rotting body' as he struggles to answer his own question, 'If a man dies, will he live again?' (Job 14:14).

Life's brief span

Some time ago I recall watching a television programme on the subject 'Death Education'. Children in some American schools at the primary level were being taught to understand death and dying. The thinking behind it was that during the course of a year the average American child sees around 10,000 fictional deaths on television. The trouble is, however, that the child sees no relation between these fictional killings of gangsters and Indians and the real thing when it enters the home. When Grandad or some other member of the family had died, children have been known to ask, 'Who shot him?' The aim of the educators was to familiarise children with the reality of death so as to enable them to deal with it emotionally when it entered their own experience. That is no bad thing really, since death comes to all and we need to be able to handle it emotionally when it enters the family. But what is even more important is to understand the spiritual dimension of death and to see it against the background of the brevity of man's life in this world.

Job says: 'Man born of woman is of few days and full of trouble. He springs up like a flower and withers away; like a fleeting shadow, he does not endure' (Job 14:1–2). Indeed, so brief is man's time in this world that Job finds it difficult to understand why God shows any interest in such an insignificant, impure and sinful creature. He asks: 'Do you fix your eye on

74 From despair to hope

The brevity of life

such a one? Will you bring him before you for judgment? Who can bring what is pure from the impure? No-one!' (Job 14:3–4). Furthermore, unlike God himself who is eternal, man's life has a fixed number of days. 'Man's days are determined; you have decreed the number of his months and have set limits he cannot exceed. So look away from him and let him alone, till he has put in his time like a hired man' (Job 14:5–6). As he looks at the trees of the forest Job feels that even they have more hope of longevity than man who, like a river that runs dry, has no hope of life beyond the grave:

At least there is hope for a tree: If it is cut down, it will sprout again, and its new shoots will not fail. Its roots may grow old in the ground and its stump die in the soil, yet at the scent of water it will bud and put forth shoots like a plant. But man dies and is laid low; he breathes his last and is no more. As water disappears from the sea or a river bed becomes parched and dry, so man lies down and does not rise; till the heavens are no more, men will not awake or be roused from their sleep (Job 14:7–12).

The idea that our human existence is brief and fleeting is not peculiar to Job's frame of mind at this low point in his spirits. The Bible throughout its pages is at great pains to remind us of it constantly. For the Psalmist, man's life is 'like a watch in the night … like the new grass of the morning … by evening it is dry and withered' (Psalm 90:4–6). Isaiah says that man's life is like 'a shepherd's tent … pulled down', a weaver's thread 'cut … off from the loom' (Isaiah 38:12). In the New Testament, James emphasises the ephemeral nature of life by picturing a group of businessmen engaged in forward planning and money-making, but without a thought of God in their minds. 'Now listen, you who say, "Today or tomorrow we will go to this or that city, spend a year there, carry on business and make money." Why, you do not even know what will happen tomorrow. What is your life? You are a mist that appears for a little while and then vanishes' (James 4:13–14). He is warning us against the ultimate blasphemy of leaving God out of account in the planning and direction of our little life here below, as though *we* had charge of it and knew exactly how long it would last.

Strangers in the world

If life is as brief and transient as the Bible teaches, then we need to remind

Chapter 12

ourselves that this world is not the only one that matters. We are born into this world and we live and work in this world, but we do not belong to this world. Peter addresses believers of his day as 'strangers in the world' (1 Peter 1:1). He means that we are simply passing through this world for a brief time on our way to that eternal world to which we really belong in Christ. We are pilgrims on a journey—living in time, but heirs of eternity. If we forget this, we are in grave danger—the danger of sacrificing on the altar of the 'god of this world' our noblest values of truth, honesty, goodness and spiritual integrity. In his book What is a Christian? Leonard Griffiths says he was speaking at a funeral about that 'other' world to which believers belong. Later, a businessman who was present said to him, 'The only world I believe in is this one.' Griffiths replied, 'If you did believe in another world, would it make any difference to you?' His answer was, 'Of course it would. If I believed, as you do, in another world and another life, better and more permanent than this one, I would change every major business policy I have before nightfall.'

As believers we do claim to believe in that 'other' eternal world, but does it make any real difference in our attitude to the things of this world here and now? Do we in wisdom hold loosely to the material things of this life, knowing how fragile and ephemeral they are? Some years ago an aircraft crashed in the Andes, and after seventy days in the intense cold sixteen young men belonging to a Uruguayan rugby team were rescued. One of them, Gustavo Zerbino, said that the experience had changed his scale of values. Money was once the most important thing in his life, but in the Andes he had burnt twenty-dollar and fifty-dollar bills to light a fire and keep warm. He said he was still concerned about the material things of life, but now he was concentrating more on the spiritual realities. Knowing we are 'strangers in the world' will help us to keep the material things of life in perspective. We can enjoy them, but not treat them as permanent. They belong to us only for a season, and a brief one at that, whereas the spiritual realities belong to eternity.

Making the most of time

If life and time in this world are as transient and passing as Job believed them to be, we ought as Christians to make the most of them in a positive

The brevity of life

and productive way, and not waste them on trivialities. The tendency when we are young is to think we have plenty of time and that the more serious things like prayer, worship, and our own personal relationship with Christ can be left on the back burner until a later date. But in fact the only time we have is now. As Christians we need to realise the urgency of the times in which we live and give ourselves more fully to whatever work for the gospel God has given us to do. We remember how our Lord said, 'As long as it is day, we must do the work of him who sent me. Night is coming, when no-one can work' (John 9:4).

For the Lord Jesus it was true that the night and darkness were soon to come, when his work on earth would be ended. But it is also true of us. We only have so much time in which to do God's work, and there is much to be done. There is a gospel to be preached, prayers to be prayed and a witness made, so that Christ's kingdom may be extended. There are still parts of the world that are unevangelised, and we all have family and friends still to be brought to Christ. In a day like ours we cannot afford a laid-back Christianity. The time is short, the work is urgent, and we must grasp the opportunity whilst we can.

The eternal hope

It is difficult to know what degree of light and understanding Job had with regard to the hope of a future life after death. But in the following verses the darkness in his soul momentarily disappears, as he anticipates the possibility of a future resurrection life:

If only you would hide me in the grave and conceal me till your anger has passed! If only you would set me a time and then remember me! If a man dies, will he live again? All the days of my hard service I will wait for my renewal to come. You will call and I will answer you; you will long for the creature your hands have made. Surely then you will count my steps but not keep track of my sin. My offences will be sealed up in a bag; you will cover over my sin (Job 14:13–17).

These are remarkable words. It is true that Job did not have the certainty of resurrection that we have in the fuller revelation of Christ, but the very dawning of such a hope and the yearning in his soul itself points to the truth

Chapter 12

of an afterlife. The very fact that he asks the question 'If a man dies, will he live again?' implies an instinctive craving in the human heart for life beyond the grave. The belief in the immortality of the soul, or the survival of personality beyond death, is something men have held dear for thousands of years. The ancient Egyptians believed in the survival of the spirit, which lived on as long as the survivors gave it sufficient nourishment. But Job's thinking is a distinct advance upon that. He anticipates a relationship between his present life and the life that he will one day share with God at his resurrection. 'I will wait for my renewal to come. You will call and I will answer you; you will long for the creature your hands have made' (Job 14:15). God made man for himself, and Job seems to be saying, 'If I yearn for God, then surely God yearns for me, and even death will not destroy the fellowship I have with him.'

The doctrine of resurrection and an afterlife, although not fully developed in the Old Testament, is nevertheless clearly there. Later we shall see that Job makes a further statement concerning resurrection that is even more positive than what we have in this passage: 'And after my skin has been destroyed, yet in my flesh I will see God; I myself will see him with my own eyes—I, and not another' (Job 19:26–27). Daniel too is equally positive that there is to be a resurrection both of the righteous and the wicked. 'Multitudes who sleep in the dust of the earth will awake: some to everlasting life, others to shame and everlasting contempt' (Daniel 12:2). And then there is that remarkable reference to Abraham and the sacrifice of Isaac found in Hebrews: 'By faith Abraham, when God tested him, offered Isaac as a sacrifice ... even though God had said to him, "It is through Isaac that your offspring will be reckoned." Abraham reasoned that God could raise the dead' (Hebrews 11:17–19).

All this is truly wonderful, but it still falls far short of the certainty of our hope in Christ, for Job quickly falls back into a mood of despondency. 'But as a mountain erodes and crumbles and as a rock is moved from its place, as water wears away stones and torrents wash away the soil, so you destroy man's hope ... He feels but the pain of his own body and mourns only for himself' (Job 14:18–22). The vision of the glorious future had faded, and Job was left only with the pain of the present. And so it is with all those who do not have the certainty of resurrection life in Christ. Men may have from time to time their 'Intimations of Immortality' as Wordsworth says, but all too soon the 'vision splendid fades into the light of common day'. Only the Christian believer can answer Job's question 'If a man dies, will he live again?' with the positive affirmation Christ himself gives us: 'I am the resurrection and the life. He who believes in me will live, even though he dies; and whoever lives and believes in me will never die' (John 11:25).

But even with that certain promise of a future resurrection coming from Christ himself, we believers are not free to criticise Job for falling back into a mood of despondency following his assertion of an afterlife. For we ourselves do not always live daily in the assurance of our resurrection faith, and pain and misery can quickly darken our hope just as it did with Job. There is a story that, during the height of the Reformation, Martin Luther on one occasion found his wife Katarina dressed in deep mourning and asked her who was dead, only to receive the reply, 'God is'. He was deeply shocked and angry at her irreverence, until she explained that his recent mood of despondency and depression sent out that message to everyone. Is that the message we are sending out to the secular man when we hit hard times—that ours is a dead Saviour who can give us no greater hope than the ideologies and false gods of man's own making? Job, in that far-off age, had greater reason than we have for the doubt that may have darkened his hope. For we know that Christ is alive, and the same power that brought him from the dead is operating in us as we live our lives in the face of the pressures and tensions of today's world.

Chapter 13

What is man?

Read Job chapter 15

The first cycle of dialogues between Job and his friends has now ended and Eliphaz opens this second round of speeches with a really vicious verbal attack upon Job's spiritual integrity. 'Then Eliphaz the Temanite replied: "Would a wise man answer with empty notions or fill his belly with the hot east wind? Would he argue with useless words, with speeches that have no value? But you even undermine piety and hinder devotion to God. Your sin prompts your mouth; you adopt the tongue of the crafty. Your own mouth condemns you, not mine; your own lips testify against you"' (Job 15:1–6).

Failure in patience

Those are cruel words by Eliphaz, especially as they are not true of Job. At the beginning of the book, when Eliphaz made his first speech, he appeared to be the most sympathetic and helpful of the friends. But his attitude has now changed. He is most abusive and contemptuous in his manner. It is as though he has lost all patience with Job and has become thoroughly exasperated with him; (probably) because Job had refused to accept the advice he and his friends had given him. He says that Job may have the reputation of being a wise man, but in fact he is no more than a 'windbag' full of empty notions and hot air. He further condemns him as a hypocrite because he masquerades as a man of piety, whereas in fact his secret sin and the irreverent things he has said about God testify against him. All this is terribly vindictive and tells us more about Eliphaz's lack of patience and wounded pride than it does about Job.

This must surely ring a bell with us. We find it so hard to be patient at times when dealing with others. And we excuse ourselves by thinking that it is all to do with natural temperament, that some are born with a more gracious and patient nature than others. But the Bible says nothing about that. What it does say is that patience is a fruit of the Spirit (Galatians 5:22) and can be cultivated like any other fruit. This cultivation becomes very

What is man?

necessary when dealing with other people concerning the things of God. What was so infuriating and exasperating to Eliphaz was Job's seeming inability to understand or grasp the great truths, as he thought, which he and his friends had been expressing. He says as much in verses 11 and 13. 'Are God's consolations not enough for you, words spoken gently to you? Why has your heart carried you away, and why do your eyes flash, so that you vent your rage against God and pour out such words from your mouth?' When I read the Gospels I get the feeling that the slowness and dullness of the disciples to grasp what Jesus was saying must have been infuriating at times. But, unlike Eliphaz, our Lord was very patient with them and would repeat the same thing again and again.

We can so easily become frustrated and impatient with people's blindness to God's truth, especially when we have been witnessing to them for some considerable time. 'Why can't they see it?' we ask ourselves. 'It is all so perfectly clear.' But is it so clear? Remember, 'the god of this age has blinded the minds of unbelievers, so that they cannot see the light of the gospel of the glory of Christ' (2 Corinthians 4:4). It is not simply the dullness of the human mind that we are contending with but 'the spiritual forces of evil in the heavenly realms' (Ephesians 6:12). We must bear patiently with people, therefore, until God himself by the Holy Spirit opens the eyes of the understanding and brings them to repentance and faith.

Hindrances to devotion

But the unkindest cut of all was the accusation of Eliphaz that Job had deliberately undermined faith and devotion in himself, and was a discouragement and hindrance to the faith of others. 'But you even undermine piety and hinder devotion to God' (Job 15:4). That was certainly not true. What Eliphaz did not know was that the depth of Job's devotion was the very reason that God had chosen his life to be the battleground for faith in the first place. Nevertheless the charge Eliphaz makes can be true of us if we are not careful. We may see clearly enough how easy it is to undermine our own spirituality through neglect of prayer, and the reading of God's Word, and the encouragement and upbuilding which comes from regular worship and fellowship with God's people. But are we sufficiently aware of how easily we can become a hindrance and

Chapter 13

stumbling block to the faith and devotion of those around us? The truth is, what we do and how we live can exercise a considerable influence on others. Even though we may not know it, someone—perhaps a younger or weaker Christian—is taking his or her cue from us, and our behaviour can profoundly affect their faith. Paul deals with this very problem in his letters to the Romans and Corinthians when speaking of the relationship between the strong and the weak Christian. 'Be careful, however, that the exercise of your freedom does not become a stumbling-block to the weak' (1 Corinthians 8:9). He means that whilst my freedom in Christ allows me to engage in a course of action which in no way troubles my conscience, nevertheless it may encourage another person, who does have scruples about it, to do that very thing and thereby violate his conscience and undermine his faith. So the ruling principle must always be not simply my liberty in Christ to satisfy my own desires, but my liberty combined with a love for fellow believers.

Spiritual insight

We sense the rising anger in Eliphaz's tone as he continues to interrogate Job with a series of sarcastic questions; 'Are you the first man ever born? Were you brought forth before the hills? Do you listen in on God's council? Do you limit wisdom to yourself? What do you know that we do not know? What insights do you have that we do not have? The grey-haired and the aged are on our side, men even older than your father' (Job 15:7–10). He tries to put Job down. He says in effect: 'Who do you think you are to claim a monopoly of wisdom? Are you so ancient and wise that you existed before the hills and have a place in the secret councils of God? Let me tell you Job, you know no more than we do. What is more, antiquity is on our side and our point of view is supported by the wisdom of the past.'

To be fair to Job, he never had claimed to have a monopoly on wisdom; and it was probably true, as Eliphaz says, that at the human level of knowledge Job did not know any more than his friends. But when Eliphaz says, 'What insights do you have that we do not have?' he is on weaker ground. For it is evident from what has been said already by both parties that Job, in spite of his more intemperate statements, did in fact have a deeper spiritual insight. Eliphaz and his friends were trapped in their rigid and simplistic system of belief concerning the doctrine of double retribution—God always blesses the righteous, and always punishes the wicked. Therefore it was impossible for them to accept that Job's sufferings could be due to anything, other than the fact that he was a great sinner. It was inconceivable to their mindset that a godly man could experience such misery and lose everything as had happened to Job.

They were right in thinking that a world ruled and governed by a just and holy God must have within it a place for rewards and punishments; but they were wrong to assume that God's way of doing things is the same as ours, or that God's mind is like our mind. God is a very complicated being, in the sense that he is sovereign and says of himself, 'For my thoughts are not your thoughts, neither are your ways my ways' (Isaiah 55:8). Like Eliphaz, we like things to be uncomplicated and easy to understand, but religious faith is not always like that. There is a dimension of God's being that is inscrutable to us, and it is not surprising therefore that we should find it perplexing and frustrating at times when we try to understand his ways with us. As for the wisdom of antiquity that Eliphaz claimed supported their viewpoint, that certainly cannot be relied upon. History is littered with the tragedies brought about by the stupidities of man. Furthermore, whilst we should learn from the mistakes of the past and each of us should become wiser as we grow older, experience testifies that that is not always the case.

Job on the other hand, out of his own inner struggle, was gaining an ever deeper insight into the character and ways of God. He was confused and perplexed concerning God's dealings with him, but all the time he was learning truths that God was teaching him, truths that he did not know before. This is borne out at the end of the book, when God says to Eliphaz and his friends: 'I am angry with you and your two friends, because you have not spoken of me what is right, as my servant Job has' (Job 42:7). We learn from all this that there is an insight and spiritual understanding that are open to all believers and have nothing to do with a person's intellectual ability. It is what James calls 'the wisdom that comes from heaven' (James 3:17). Paul urges Timothy: 'Reflect on what I am saying, for the Lord will give you insight into all this' (2 Timothy 2:7). This spiritual perception comes with the growing desire to know the truth. It is God-given through

Chapter 13

the Holy Spirit and is only for the believer, for he alone has the Spirit of God within him.

This whole question of insight and wisdom will be dealt with more fully when we come to chapter 28, where Job's discourse is concerned with answering just one question: 'But where can wisdom be found?'

What is man?

In the final section of this chapter Eliphaz, still with Job in mind, poses a very important question: 'What is man, that he could be pure, or one born of woman, that he could be righteous? If God places no trust in his holy ones, if even the heavens are not pure in his eyes, how much less man, who is vile and corrupt, who drinks up evil like water!' (Job 15:4–16). Eliphaz is in no doubt that Job is impure; he 'drinks up evil like water', and that is why God is punishing him. He is definitely wrong where Job is concerned, but the question itself is a valid one when applied to mankind in general. What is man? The Bible gives two answers to that, both of which are right, and both of which are needed if we are to understand human nature in its relation to God.

First, there is the answer of Eliphaz, that man is vile and corrupt and drinks up evil like water. He expands on this from verse 17 to the end of the chapter, describing the wickedness of man in a variety of figures of speech. Here are some of the main points he makes. Man has to live with the daily consequences of his sinful deeds through a guilty conscience (Job 15:20–23). He experiences no lasting peace because he knows that his rebellion will one day bring God's judgement upon him (Job 15:24–26). He may enjoy the good life and fat living here and now, but a day is coming when it will all disappear and, like a vine stripped bare, he will stand naked before the judgement of God except for his immortal soul (Job 15:27–35). In answer to his question 'What is man?' Eliphaz is right to stress the sinful aspect of human nature, and in this he is in harmony with the rest of the Bible and with the gospel of Christ. Apart from God and the salvation he provided, man is lost and hopeless, and heading for eternal destruction.

Second, in answer to the question 'What is man?' we must also look again to the answer given by the Psalmist. 'When I consider your heavens, the work of your fingers, the moon and the stars, which you have set in place, what is man that you are mindful of him, the son of man that you care for him? You made him a little lower than the heavenly beings and crowned him with glory and honour' (Psalm 8:3–5). As he views the immensity of the heavens, the Psalmist is filled with wonder and gratitude that God gives man more attention than all the rest of creation. This is because God had imbued man with soul and spirit and made him a little lower than the angels, crowning him with glory and honour. Here is an echo of Genesis 1:27, where we read: 'So God created man in his own image … male and female he created them.' All this spells out that man has a special dignity and a special place in the scheme of things. And this is where his hope lies, in the fact that he is able to correspond with God and to know God's love towards him. He is a sinner, yes. He is lost and hopeless and cannot save himself, yes. But he is also a living soul and precious in God's sight—so precious indeed that he gave his own Son to redeem man and to reconcile him to himself.

Chapter 14

Miserable comforters

Read Job chapters 16 and 17

At the beginning of the book of Job, when the friends heard of his troubles, they visited Job and attempted to comfort him. They were genuinely distressed at the change in him and expressed their feelings in the manner of the time. 'When they saw him from a distance, they could hardly recognise him; they began to weep aloud, and they tore their robes and sprinkled dust on their heads' (Job 2:12). But all that was to change, as they and Job disputed God's dealings with him. Again and again they charged him with bringing God's judgement upon himself because of his sin, so that what was intended originally to be a ministry of friendship and comfort degenerated into an interrogation, with Job at the receiving end.

Friendship and comfort

Chapter 16 opens with Job expressing his disappointment that his friends had failed him in the hour of need. 'Then Job replied: "I have heard many things like these; miserable comforters are you all! Will your long-winded speeches never end? What ails you that you keep on arguing? I also could speak like you, if you were in my place; I could make fine speeches against you and shake my head at you. But my mouth would encourage you; comfort from my lips would bring you relief' (Job 16:1–5). Job's chief complaint is that, instead of exercising a ministry of friendship and comfort in trying to understand why he is suffering in the way he is, they have simply assumed that he must be guilty of some great sin. If the roles were reversed and they were in his place, then he would at least try to comfort and relieve them in their distress, and not just shake his head disapprovingly as though his situation were hopeless.

Job's outburst is understandable. In times of trouble we all need, and have a right to expect, comfort and encouragement from those who claim to be our friends. The Bible has a great deal to say about the quality of true friendship. The story of David and Jonathan is an illustration of all that friendship at the deepest level should be. The book of Proverbs is full of observations on the nature of friendship: 'A friend loves at all times' (Proverbs 17:17); 'there is a friend who sticks closer than a brother' (Proverbs 18:24); 'Wounds from a friend can be trusted' (Proverbs 27:6). From John's Gospel we learn what our Lord Jesus meant by friendship: 'Greater love has no-one than this, that he lay down his life for his friends. You are my friends if you do what I command. I no longer call you servants, because a servant does not know his master's business. Instead, I have called you friends, for everything that I learned from my Father I have made known to you' (John 15:13–15).

Like others, the Christian too needs a close friend, apart, that is, from the general fellowship he enjoys with other believers. In such a friendship there is a kinship of spirit that is close and intimate, making it possible to talk and share at the deepest level without the risk of being laughed at or having our deepest feelings trivialised. All this surely was in our Lord's mind when he said, 'I no longer call you servants ... [but] friends'. The closeness of our relationship with him means he shares with us the secrets of his kingdom, and we in turn can confide in him the hopes and fears we could never share with anyone else.

True friendship can stand the strain of genuine criticism and being told one's faults. That is the meaning of the proverb quoted above: 'Wounds from a friend can be trusted, but an enemy multiplies kisses' (Proverbs 27:6). A true friend will expose our mistakes and indiscretions not in order to hurt, but to help. On the other hand, the so-called 'friend' who, whatever our feelings, is all flattery and kisses, can truly destroy us. We have only to think of the kiss of Judas to see the truth of that. Christ calls us his friends, and he wounds us, chastises us and rebukes us through the truth of his Word, but only because he loves us and desires us to know the fullness of our salvation.

Finally, the Christian believer needs to be careful in his choice of friends. We must of course be friendly with everyone, including the non-Christian. But it seems to me impossible that a true believer can have any kind of close intimate friendship with a non-believer. After all, as Christian brothers and sisters we have certain shared experiences from which the non-Christian is excluded. We share in the regenerating power of the Holy Spirit in our lives,

Chapter 14

we have the same hope of heaven in our hearts, and we accept the same authority of God's Word in the Holy Scriptures. These are the things that give an added dimension to our friendship as Christians. As the hymn says:

> Blest be the tie that binds
> Our hearts in Christian love;
> The fellowship of kindred minds
> Is like to that above.

Why does God have to spoil everything?

With the failure of his friends to give him any real comfort or to show any true understanding of his position, Job lapses further into despondency in the remaining verses of chapter 16 and through chapter 17. And yet it is not all unrelieved gloom. There are flashes of light in the darkness, showing us that Job has not lost his faith in spite of his inner writhing and torment.

He first complains that neither his speech nor his silence brings any sense of spiritual relief, because God seems intent on making him suffer. 'Yet if I speak, my pain is not relieved; and if I refrain, it does not go away. Surely, O God, you have worn me out; you have devastated my entire household. You have bound me—and it has become a witness; my gauntness rises up and testifies against me. God assails me and tears me in his anger and gnashes his teeth at me; my opponent fastens on me his piercing eyes' (Job 16:6–9). He depicts God as a savage beast tearing at his flesh in anger. He even feels that God has deliberately handed him over to wicked men, for them to do as they liked with him: 'Men open their mouths to jeer at me; they strike my cheek in scorn and unite together against me. God has turned me over to evil men and thrown me into the clutches of the wicked' (Job 16:10–11). This is daring language—to accuse God of joining forces with the wicked in attacking him!

And then comes the bitterest complaint of all. Why did God have to spoil everything? 'All was well with me, but he shattered me; he seized me by the neck and crushed me. He has made me his target; his archers surround me. Without pity, he pierces my kidneys and spills my gall on the ground. Again and again he bursts upon me, he rushes at me like a warrior' (Job 16:12–14).

Miserable comforters

In this, another forceful word-picture, Job sees God as a fierce archer who deliberately shoots his arrows at him as a target in order to increase his suffering. And all this, says Job, in spite of the fact that 'my hands have been free of violence and my prayer is pure' (Job 16:17).

We can sympathise with Job, because it can be our experience that everything in life seems to be going well at one moment—our marriage and home life, our work and our devotional life—and then suddenly something devastating happens and our life is blown apart. And when this happens, like Job, we are tempted to lash out at God in our hurt and frustration and feel that he is to blame. And in one sense he is to blame, since it is he who allows these dreadful things to happen to us. That is clear from the opening chapters of the book of Job. Satan is the instigator of Job's misery, but only because he is under God's direction. But 'blame' is not the best word in this context, since it generally means to accuse someone of wrongdoing, and that cannot be true of God. This indeed is one of the major themes of the book of Job: how to relate the presence of suffering in the world with the righteous, loving character of God. Job wrestles, as we all have to do, on the one hand with the temptation to demand a rational explanation from God, and on the other with the challenge simply to trust him absolutely.

Although we cannot give an adequate explanation of undeserved suffering, the Bible is clear that there are reasons why we need not allow it to undermine our faith in God. There is the solid promise that nothing that happens to us in this life can ever separate us from God's love: 'Who shall separate us from the love of Christ? Shall trouble or hardship or persecution or famine or nakedness or danger or sword? ... No, in all these things we are more than conquerors through him who loved us' (Romans 8:35,37). We can sometimes serve God best through our suffering, as the history of world mission clearly shows: 'The seed must die if it is to multiply.' Suffering can be the means whereby we grow in holiness and our faith is purified and strengthened: 'you may have had to suffer grief in all kinds of trials. These have come so that your faith—of greater worth than gold, which perishes even though refined by fire—may be proved genuine and may result in praise, glory and honour when Jesus Christ is revealed' (1 Peter 1:6–7). Suffering can also have a disciplinary purpose in the life of

Chapter 14

the Christian, to teach us some lesson God wants us to learn or to draw us back to himself when we have strayed from him.

In all this we must never forget the role of sin in relation to the problem of suffering. The New Testament writers regard death and the suffering associated with it as an alien intrusion into God's world: 'sin entered the world through one man, and death through sin, and in this way death came to all men, because all sinned' (Romans 5:12). So, whether we like it or not, we are part of a human system in which sin underlies all the evils and suffering which afflict mankind. God's answer to sin was the death of Christ on the cross, where he died our death and bore the penalty of our sin. The only meaningful response to suffering, therefore, is to see it from the vantage point of the cross. This puts it in its proper perspective and helps us to bear it with courage and hope.

An advocate on high

We said earlier that in spite of his mood of despondency in chapters 16 and 17, there are flashes of light which illuminate the darkness and show us that Job has not lost his faith. Here is the first of these: 'O earth, do not cover my blood; may my cry never be laid to rest! Even now my witness is in heaven, my advocate is on high. My intercessor is my friend as my eyes pour out tears to God; on behalf of a man he pleads with God as a man pleads with his friend' (Job 16:18–21). These are remarkable words. Job is saying that even after his death the truth of his innocence will be vindicated before God, as his blood will cry out from the ground like that of Abel's in the Genesis story (Genesis 4:10). More than that, he believes that in heaven there is one who will be his advocate and intercessor to plead his cause before God. Job's understanding of an advocate on high may have been dim and clouded, but in a wonderfully prophetic way he is pointing forward to what is a certainty for the Christian believer. For we do have an advocate on high in the person of Christ. 'My dear children, I write this to you so that you will not sin. But if anybody does sin, we have one who speaks to the Father in our defence—Jesus Christ, the Righteous One' (1 John 2:1).

We may wonder why the believer needs an advocate or someone to speak in his defence before God. Isn't it enough that we are Christians and children of our heavenly Father? Doesn't that settle once and for all our relationship with God? John answered that clearly in 1 John 1:8 'If we claim to be without sin, we deceive ourselves and the truth is not in us.' Even when we have been born of God's Spirit, sin is a continuing reality in our lives. We are always having to struggle with the world, the flesh and the devil; and when we stumble and fall into sin, Christ is the one who pleads our cause before the Father and restores our fellowship with him.

Perseverance of the saints

As we move into chapter 17, the atmosphere of doleful despair is still present, but it is not all gloom and darkness, as we shall see. Job's thoughts turn once again to death and the grave. 'My spirit is broken, my days are cut short, the grave awaits me. Surely mockers surround me; my eyes must dwell on their hostility' (Job 17:1–2). He asks that God himself will provide a guarantee or pledge of his innocence in the face of the charges of his friends. 'Give me, O God, the pledge you demand. Who else will put up security for me? You have closed their minds to understanding; therefore you will not let them triumph. If a man denounces his friends for reward, the eyes of his children will fail. God has made me a byword to everyone, a man in whose face people spit' (Job 17:3–6). His sense of anger and hopelessness comes out very strongly in his rejection of his friends' facile and superficial optimism, as they claim that the darkness will soon be passed and he will once again come out into the light. 'These men turn night into day; in the face of darkness they say, "Light is near." If the only home I hope for is the grave, if I spread out my bed in darkness, if I say to corruption, "You are my father," and to the worm, "My mother" or "My sister", where then is my hope? Who can see any hope for me?' (Job 17:12–15).

In all that we hear echoes of the way in which people today might say, 'Cheer up! It isn't that bad!' or 'Look on the sunny side' or 'Every cloud has a silver lining', and so on. When one's heart is breaking, such facile optimism is heartless and cruel. What is more, those who adopt that kind of superficial cheerfulness are themselves in a bad way, because they are refusing to face up to the stark, brutal realities of life, which cannot be changed simply by pretending they are not there. We need something much stronger and deeper than that to keep us going when we feel like giving up.

Chapter 14

And that is where Job's faith comes to light up his darkness: 'Nevertheless, the righteous will hold to their ways, and those with clean hands will grow stronger' (Job 17:9).

He is hanging in there and is confident that, with God's help, he will see his way through the darkness, and will even come out with a faith stronger than before. In New Testament language that would be the equivalent of the doctrine of the perseverance of the saints. As Paul puts it, 'I thank my God every time I remember you … being confident of this, that he who began a good work in you will carry it on to completion until the day of Christ Jesus' (Philippians 1:3–6). The 'good work' is God's work of salvation in our lives, which he initiated in Christ and which he will continue to bring to completion one day in our heavenly home. Being a Christian in today's world can certainly be difficult and problematic at times, and we all feel occasionally like giving in and giving up. But God will not allow that. We find it easy to start things, and equally easy to give them up. But God is not like us. When he starts something he always finishes it. And where our salvation is concerned he put a stubborn perseverance in our hearts, which persists and keeps us going in the Christian way even when things are as black with us as they were with Job.

Chapter 15

The doom of the wicked

Read Job chapter 18

In the second round of dialogue Bildad now weighs in with his contribution to the discussion. What Job had said earlier in chapters 16 and 17 about the friends being 'miserable comforters' had clearly rattled Bildad. 'When will you end these speeches? Be sensible, and then we can talk. Why are we regarded as cattle and considered stupid in your sight?' (Job 18:2–3). The picture he may have had in mind is the way sheep and cows stand and stare vacantly. W. H. Davies, the Welsh tramp poet, uses the same imagery in one of his poems:

> What is this life if, full of care,
> We have no time to stand and stare?
> No time to stand beneath the boughs
> And stare as long as sheep or cows?

Bildad seems to have been a bit 'touchy' in his attitude. Although Job had used some strong language towards his friends, he had never at any time accused them of dumb stupidity.

Anger—right or wrong?

Bildad is much nearer the mark when he says that Job's emotional reaction is almost hysterical. 'You who tear yourself to pieces in your anger, is the earth to be abandoned for your sake? Or must the rocks be moved from their place?' (Job 18:4). There he puts his finger on what has been a weakness in Job's response to what has happened to him. Bildad says in effect: 'You get yourself all emotionally worked up, tearing yourself to pieces in your anger against God as if that is going to change the way God does things. Do you think God is going to turn the whole creation upside down, change his laws and remove the rocks from their place, just to suit your way of thinking? No, you must learn that anger, especially towards God, is a destructive emotion, and the only person it tears in pieces is yourself.'

From despair to hope **93**

Chapter 15

Bildad, of course, was quite right in what he said. But we need not elaborate on it now, since we dealt with the destructive effects of resentment and anger when looking at Eliphaz's speech in Job 5:1–2. But as we are dealing with this subject we need to remind ourselves that there is a right kind of anger in the Christian life. This is exemplified in the life of Jesus. In Mark's Gospel we read of Jesus healing a man on the Sabbath day in the face of the hostility of the Pharisees. 'He looked round at them in anger and, deeply distressed at their stubborn hearts, said to the man, "Stretch out your hand." He stretched it out, and his hand was completely restored' (Mark 3:5). An even clearer illustration of our Lord's anger is his treatment of the money-changers in the temple. 'So he made a whip out of cords, and drove all from the temple area, both sheep and cattle; he scattered the coins of the money-changers and overturned their tables. To those who sold doves he said, "Get these out of here! How dare you turn my Father's house into a market!"' (John 2:15–16).

That must have been a terrible sight, to see the Lamb of God with a whip in his hand and his eyes blazing with anger. It tells us that we dare not sentimentalise about the Lord Jesus. Just as he would not tolerate contempt for holy things then, so he will not tolerate the secularisation and commercialisation of God's house and the trivialisation of God's truth today. There is, therefore, a right kind of anger that needs to be expressed by the people of God. It is not the kind that flares up in a moment and causes havoc in a household and tears away at our own emotions. Nor is it the kind that expresses itself in private petulance and irascibility over petty things. All that is totally inexcusable in a Christian. But it is the kind of anger that is best described as a 'holy passion' against all the abuses of sin and tyranny and anything that causes human suffering in the world. Anger is an emotion that needs careful handling; it is only right when it glorifies God and is directed at Satan and the forces of darkness.

The hopelessness of godlessness

In the remainder of the chapter Bildad turns to a familiar theme: the doom of the wicked, or the hopelessness of the man without God. Did he have Job in mind, we wonder? However that may be, his language is full of vivid poetic imagery, which serves to emphasise the truths he is teaching about

The doom of the wicked

the fate of the wicked—truths which are to be found in other parts of the Bible.

His first image is of the godless man in a state of darkness. 'The lamp of the wicked is snuffed out; the flame of his fire stops burning. The light in his tent becomes dark; the lamp beside him goes out. The vigour of his step is weakened, his own schemes throw him down' (Job 18:5–7). Without God in his life, a man is like someone in a tent whose lamp suddenly flickers, plunging him into darkness. He tries to move around, but his steps get confused and he stumbles and falls down. Our Lord used the same imagery: 'I am the light of the world. Whoever follows me will never walk in darkness, but will have the light of life' (John 8:12). Also Paul: 'For you were once darkness, but now you are light in the Lord' (Ephesians 5:8). Some would view this picture of man stumbling along in darkness as a gloomy, pessimistic description. Modern man, they say, is an enlightened individual; he has great knowledge and understanding, and he has made great progress in learning, exploration, discovery and the application of knowledge in modern technology. We would agree with that. Man is an enlightened being, and we thank God for all the advances made in medicine, transportation and living standards. But with it all, he is still in a state of spiritual and moral darkness. He still does not realise the value of his soul; he rejects the hope of heaven and persists in disregarding the laws and commands of God. The result is that he stumbles along in this life without direction, and brings all kinds of evil upon himself.

In his second image Bildad sees the godless man stumbling along in the darkness from one disaster to another:

His feet thrust him into a net and he wanders into its mesh. A trap seizes him by the heel; a snare holds him fast. A noose is hidden for him on the ground; a trap lies in his path. Terrors startle him on every side and dog his every step. Calamity is hungry for him; disaster is ready for him when he falls. It eats away parts of his skin; death's firstborn devours his limbs. He is torn from the security of his tent and marched off to the king of terrors. Fire resides in his tent; burning sulphur is scattered over his dwelling (Job 18:8–15).

That is a picture of man and his world in a state of continual crisis, because

Chapter 15

he has rejected God's direction and has nothing to put in its place. In a speech made at the Guildhall, London, in October 1989, Mrs Thatcher, the then Prime Minister, acknowledged how disappointed she was at the failure of vastly improved living standards to eradicate such social evils as child cruelty, violence, terrorism and drug addiction in our country. 'For years, when I was young and in politics with all the hopes and dreams and ambitions, it seemed to me that if we got an age where we had good housing, good education, a reasonable standard of living, then everything would be set fair and we should have an easier future. We know now that that isn't so. We're up against the real problems of human nature.' The Prime Minister did not go on to ask the question, What is the problem of human nature? But the Bible is clear: man stumbles along in the darkness and blindness of his own sin.

In his last piece of imagery Bildad pictures the final destruction of the godless man or woman under the judgement of God: 'His roots dry up below and his branches wither above. The memory of him perishes from the earth; he has no name in the land. He is driven from light into darkness and is banished from the world. He has no offspring or descendants among his people, no survivor where once he lived. Men of the west are appalled at his fate; men of the east are seized with horror. Surely such is the dwelling of an evil man; such is the place of one who knows not God' (Job 18:16–21). Like a withered-up tree, the wicked man, cut off from the source of life in God, is headed for destruction. He is forgotten by this world and, in the next, he is cast into the darkness of eternal death. Making allowances for the imagery, the truth Bildad is teaching is not very different from the teaching of the gospel. Without the water of life that Christ offers for the deep thirst of the human soul, man is an unsatisfied being, the victim of a vague discontent and inward dryness that he does not understand. That surely was the message of our Lord to the woman of Samaria: 'whoever drinks the water I give him will never thirst. Indeed, the water I give him will become in him a spring of water welling up to eternal life' (John 4:14). The heart that is filled with God's fullness becomes itself the resource of a new life of blessing and power. But, apart from God, man is both empty and lost. Speaking of death and the underworld Bildad says, 'he is driven from light into darkness', and again and again in his parables our Lord speaks of the lost soul being cast 'into the darkness, where there will be weeping and gnashing of teeth' (Matthew 8:12; 22:13).

Chapter 16

The triumph of faith

Read Job chapter 19

This is a chapter that begins with Job continuing in a deep low, but it ends with him riding on a great high. In response to Bildad and the other friends his opening words reflect the deep hurt he feels in his soul and spirit because of the unjust criticism and judgmental attacks the friends have levelled at him. 'Then Job replied: 'How long will you torment me and crush me with words? Ten times now you have reproached me; shamelessly you attack me. If it is true that I have gone astray, my error remains my concern alone. If indeed you would exalt yourselves above me and use my humiliation against me, then know that God has wronged me and drawn his net around me' (Job 19:1–6).

Personal responsibility

Because we know the reason for Job's suffering we cannot help feeling as incensed as he was that his friends should adopt such a spiritually superior attitude in treating him as a great sinner. He tells them that if they want to 'exalt' themselves and 'humiliate' him, then they had better realise that it is God they are dealing with and not himself alone. 'Furthermore,' he says in effect, 'what right have you to judge me? If I have sinned and gone astray, then that is a matter for myself and God alone. You are in no position to know my heart and judge my true condition. Only God can do that.'

He is perfectly right, of course. Every one of us is personally responsible for the state of his own soul before God; no one can take that responsibility from us, nor can we put it on anyone else. And yet, right from the beginning of time, man's instinct has been to avoid personal responsibility for his own sins. When Adam fell into sin and God challenged him, his reply was: 'The woman you put here with me—she gave me some fruit from the tree, and I ate it' (Genesis 3:12). In the same way, when God questioned Eve, she shifted the responsibility on to the serpent. 'Then the Lord God said to the woman, "What is this you have done?" The woman said, "The serpent deceived me, and I ate"' (Genesis 3:13). This failure to accept responsibility for our actions has become almost a national hobby today. More and more we hear the plea of 'diminished responsibility' being echoed in the lawcourts as the perpetrators of crime shift the blame on to their poor upbringing, or drink, or the lack of educational opportunities. Job at least is prepared to acknowledge that his sin or error is a matter for him alone to sort out with God, as it is with everyone else.

The secret side of things

There is another aspect to all this, and we need to remind ourselves of it. The friends made the mistake of thinking they knew the real Job: they did not. That is why he tells them not to 'torment' and 'crush' him with their words of reproach, as if they knew the secret places of his soul. Who are they to judge him as if they were God, who alone knows the hidden things in the depths of our being? This is a truth the Scriptures deal with again and again. 'The Lord does not look at the things man looks at. Man looks at the outward appearance, but the Lord looks at the heart' (1 Samuel 16: 7). Or take our Lord's words about prayer: 'When you pray, go into your room, close the door and pray to your Father, who is unseen. Then your Father, who sees what is done in secret, will reward you' (Matthew 6:6). It is not so much the secret place that is important in prayer as the secret 'inner' disposition of heart and mind. We are inwardly alone with God, shutting out the world. Paul says to the Colossians, 'For you died, and your life is now hidden with Christ in God' (Colossians 3:3). The life of the believer, then, is in this sense a secret hidden life, hidden from the world, hidden even from other Christians, but known to God both in its weaknesses and its strengths.

When no one cares

One of the most dreadful experiences in all the world is when we reach a point in our lives, because of circumstances, when we feel that no one cares about us, neither God nor man. As we continue through the next section it seems that Job has reached that point. First, it is God who does not care.

Though I cry, 'I've been wronged!' I get no response; though I call for help, there is no justice. He has blocked my way so that I cannot pass … He has stripped me of my

Chapter 16

honour and removed the crown from my head. He tears me down on every side till I am gone; he uproots my hope like a tree. His anger burns against me; he counts me among his enemies. His troops advance in force; they build a siege ramp against me and encamp around my tent (Job 19:7–12).

Job feels trapped in his situation like a city under siege, and even God does not care when he calls to heaven for help.

Psalm 46 begins: 'God is our refuge and strength, an ever-present help in trouble.' H. G. Wells in one of his most bitter moments parodied that verse and complained, 'God is an ever-absent help in trouble.' We may never have reached that depth of cynicism, but, like Job, we may well have felt at times that we have cried out to God in prayer, and that he either has not heard or he does not care. But neither is true. He does care, whatever we feel to the contrary. The fact is that we ought to rely less on our feelings and more on the truth of God's Word. Feelings are unreliable; they change from one moment to the next. But God has given us his Word and he cares, and we can depend on that. 'Cast all your anxiety on him because he cares for you' (1 Peter 5:7). Furthermore, God always hears our prayers even if he does not always answer them as quickly as we want or in the way we want. Job's own experience is a commentary on that fact. He had to wait God's own time for him to act, but act he did, and at the end Job's life was more blessed than at the beginning. So let us not give up on prayer as though it were a waste of time. Our Lord said we 'should always pray and not give up' (Luke 18:1).

Second, the situation was aggravated because Job also felt that other people did not care.

He has alienated my brothers from me; my acquaintances are completely estranged from me. My kinsmen have gone away; my friends have forgotten me. My guests and my maidservants count me a stranger; they look upon me as an alien. I summon my servant, but he does not answer, though I beg him with my own mouth. My breath is offensive to my wife; I am loathsome to my own brothers. Even the little boys scorn me; when I appear they ridicule me. All my intimate friends detest me; those I love have turned against me. I am nothing but skin and bones; I have escaped by only the skin of my teeth. Have pity on me, my friends, have pity, for the hand of God has struck me. Why do you pursue me as God does? Will you never get enough of my flesh? (Job 19:13–22).

The triumph of faith

That is a sad picture, and it tells us more about human frailty, and the weakness of human love and friendship, than about Job. His diseased body had made him offensive to others, even to his own wife and family, and his skeletal frame caused little boys to poke fun at him. But Job was to learn one very important lesson out of all this, and it comes out in the next section. Whereas all other loves and friendships fail and let us down, the love of God in Christ is dependable and lasting. Like Job, George Matheson who wrote the famous hymn, 'O Love that wilt not let me go', says that the hymn was the result of suffering. 'The hymn was written in the manse of my former parish Innellan one summer evening in 1882. I was at the time all alone. Something had happened to me which caused me the most severe mental suffering. The hymn was the fruit of that suffering.' Whether we think of romantic love, brotherly love or mother-love, all are capable of failing us. Almost every week we read in our newspapers, or hear on the news, reports of the most dreadful forms of abuse inflicted by parents on their own children. In contrast to this failure of human love and friendship, Job suddenly, in the middle of all his complaining, comes out with a mighty statement of his personal faith in the enduring love of God.

The triumph of faith

We said at the outset that this chapter begins with Job in a deep low but ends with him riding on a great high. Well, here it is: 'Oh, that my words were recorded, that they were written on a scroll, that they were inscribed with an iron tool on lead, or engraved in rock for ever! I know that my Redeemer lives, and that in the end he will stand upon the earth. And after my skin has been destroyed, yet in my flesh I will see God; I myself will see him with my own eyes—I, and not another. How my heart yearns within me!' (Job 19:23–27).

He asks that his word of personal testimony and conviction of the love of God, and the vindication of his own innocence in the life to come, may be indelibly written as a witness to future generations of the triumph of faith over adversity. In a remarkable way that prayer was answered, since we now have that word of testimony in the Scriptures before us. This, among other things, is an evidence surely of the veracity and imperishability of God's Word in Scripture.

Chapter 16

But the testimony itself is also remarkable. Job is not uttering some vague wish or some idle thought about God, but speaks out of deep personal conviction. 'I know that my Redeemer lives.' Many people today have a vague belief in God as some kind of remote intelligence or cosmic mind, but if you were to ask them if they know God personally as Redeemer, Saviour, Father and Friend they would not have the slightest notion what you were talking about. Yet this is what stands out in Job's testimony. He knows God personally as a living Redeemer, and he is convinced that when this life is done, his emaciated body will be restored and he will see God and live in his presence. He may not have known the full import of his words, but in this remarkable way he is anticipating the resurrection of Christ and the bodily resurrection of the believer: 'in my flesh I will see God'. This is no different from what Paul says to the Corinthians: 'I declare to you, brothers, that flesh and blood cannot inherit the kingdom of God, nor does the perishable inherit the imperishable ... For the trumpet will sound, the dead will be raised imperishable, and we will be changed' (1 Corinthians 15:50,52). This natural body will die, but when the Lord Jesus comes again to gather his own on the resurrection morning, our body will be changed into a spiritual body ready for its new home in heaven, and we shall see God and dwell in his presence. That is the promise Jesus gave: 'Blessed are the pure in heart, for they will see God' (Matthew 5:8).

The judgement

Job ends with a word of warning: 'If you say, "How we will hound him, since the root of the trouble lies in him," you should fear the sword yourselves; for wrath will bring punishment by the sword, and then you will know that there is judgment' (Job 19:28–29). He is speaking to the friends who have been so scornful and critical and have judged him wrongly. He reminds them that they will have to answer to God at the judgement for the words they have spoken. For there is a judgement of believers as well as unbelievers: 'For we must all appear before the judgment seat of Christ, that each one may receive what is due to him for the things done while in the body, whether good or bad' (2 Corinthians 5:10). As Christians we will not be judged regarding our destiny but regarding our discipleship. For the

The triumph of faith

non-Christian the warning is much more serious. The apostle Paul says: 'For he [God] has set a day when he will judge the world with justice' (Acts 17:31). That 'day' is the termination point to which all history is moving. It is the judgement day of which the Bible speaks so often, sometimes in graphic symbolic language, but always portraying a terrifying reality which will one day face the man or woman who has rejected God's salvation in Christ.

Chapter 17

Why do the wicked prosper?

Read Job chapters 20 and 21

We take these two chapters together because they both deal with the same subject—the place of the wicked in God's scheme of things. But they deal with it from opposite points of view. The speaker in chapter 20 is Zophar and he simply repeats the argument of chapter 18, so we need not spend too much time with it. With Job in mind, he maintains that the wicked always suffer in this life, and their prosperity and happiness are brief and elusive: 'Surely you know how it has been from of old, ever since man was placed on the earth, that the mirth of the wicked is brief, the joy of the godless lasts but a moment. Though his pride reaches to the heavens and his head touches the clouds, he will perish for ever, like his own dung' (Job 20:4–7). He continues in this vein right down to the closing verses, which end on the same note of the doom of the wicked: 'The heavens will expose his guilt; the earth will rise up against him. A flood will carry off his house, rushing waters on the day of God's wrath. Such is the fate God allots the wicked, the heritage appointed for them by God' (Job 20:27–29).

What Zophar is saying is not wholly wrong, but it is not wholly right either. Retribution does sometimes overtake the sinner in this life, but it is not always the case. And that is what troubles and perplexes Job as he proceeds to answer Zophar in the next chapter.

Job's problem

'Then Job replied: "Listen carefully to my words; let this be the consolation you give me. Bear with me while I speak, and after I have spoken, mock on. Is my complaint directed to man? Why should I not be impatient? Look at me and be astonished; clap your hand over your mouth. When I think about this, I am terrified; trembling seizes my body"' (Job 21:1–6). Let us paraphrase that for the moment. Job says to Zophar and the friends, 'Just bear with me a moment while I state my point of view, and then you can disagree with me or mock me. My problem or complaint is not to do with

Why do the wicked prosper?

you, Zophar, but with God, and that is why I get so impatient because God's way doesn't seem to make sense. When I tell you what my problem is, you will clap your hand over your mouth and be horrified at my daring. As a matter of fact it fills me with "trembling" when I think of what I am really saying.' So what was he saying? Well, his problem is that life and experience seem to show that instead of suffering in this life and being judged by God, the wicked often seem to prosper and God allows them to get away with it, so that in general they have a fine time.

He puts it like this:

Why do the wicked live on, growing old and increasing in power? They see their children established around them, their offspring before their eyes. Their homes are safe and free from fear; the rod of God is not upon them. Their bulls never fail to breed; their cows calve and do not miscarry. They send forth their children as a flock; their little ones dance about. They sing to the music of tambourine and harp; they make merry to the sound of the flute. They spend their years in prosperity and go down to the grave in peace. Yet they say to God, 'Leave us alone! we have no desire to know your ways. Who is the Almighty, that we should serve him? What would we gain by praying to him?' (Job 21: 7–15).

Job says in effect, 'These wicked people seem to get away with it and never suffer for their sins. If you speak to them about the things of God, they laugh in contempt and say, "Leave us alone, what do we want God for? We are doing fine without him!"'

He continues: 'It is said, "God stores up a man's punishment for his sons." Let him repay the man himself, so that he will know it. Let his own eyes see his destruction; let him drink of the wrath of the Almighty. For what does he care about the family he leaves behind when his allotted months come to an end?' (Job 21:19–21). He says to the friends, 'You say that God punishes the children for the sins of the fathers. What use is that? Why doesn't God punish them now in this life? They don't care about the children they leave behind.' He concludes by saying of the wicked man, 'He is carried to the grave, and watch is kept over his tomb. The soil in the valley is sweet to him; all men follow after him, and a countless throng goes before him' (Job 21:32–33). Even when he dies the wicked man is given a fine

From despair to hope **105**

Chapter 17

funeral, with crowds in attendance, and honours are paid to him. Job is of the opinion that what Zophar has said about the wicked always having to suffer in this life is just arrogant nonsense. He looks at his own plight, having lost health, home, family and livelihood in spite of having lived a godly life, and he says, 'So how can you console me with your nonsense? Nothing is left of your answers but falsehood!' (Job 21:34).

Our problem?

Is Job's problem ours? Do we feel at times that there is something radically wrong with the way God organises things? For there are plenty of people we know of who are exactly like those Job is describing. They are godless and totally pagan, and yet they seem to do well in this life. They cheat and steal, engage in violence and even murder, and they sell their story to the newspapers and make a million. And there are neighbours, and others we know of, who may not do any of these dreadful things, but they live their lives without a thought for God. They say in effect, 'Don't talk to us about God and religion. We don't believe in them, and yet we are doing perfectly all right. We enjoy good health, we have a nice home, our children go to a good school, and we enjoy a good standard of living. We are no worse off than those who are Christians, and in fact we are a good deal better off than many of them.' And that is what perplexes us, because what they say is often true! The Psalmist had the same problem: 'But as for me, my feet had almost slipped; I had nearly lost my foothold. For I envied the arrogant when I saw the prosperity of the wicked' (Psalm 73:2–3). He is saying that when he saw those who hold God in contempt getting on so well in this life, he almost lost his faith.

Is there an answer?

The perplexity this problem creates in our minds is the reason the book of Job was written in the first place. Not that we shall have a clear-cut answer as to why the godly suffer and the ungodly prosper, even when we get to the end of the book. But it does lay down certain principles that help us to live with this problem without losing our faith. After all, even in this chapter, in spite of his perplexity Job is certain that God is in control of the wicked and their prosperity, and therefore he himself will not follow their way of life.

Why do the wicked prosper?

'But their prosperity is not in their own hands, so I stand aloof from the counsel of the wicked' (Job 21:16).

First, we have to remember that God's mind is not like our mind. We like to have everything clear and simple and easy to understand, and we want that to be true of God. But God is not like that. He is a very complicated being, in the sense that he is the almighty and eternal God. Speaking on God's behalf, Isaiah says, 'As the heavens are higher than the earth, so are my ways higher than your ways and my thoughts than your thoughts' (Isaiah 55:9). There is therefore this mysterious hidden side to God's being, which puts him beyond the reach of our understanding when it comes to explaining why he does certain things, or allows certain things to happen in this life. The apostle Paul puts it like this: 'Oh, the depth of the riches of the wisdom and knowledge of God! How unsearchable his judgements, and his paths beyond tracing out! "Who has known the mind of the Lord? Or who has been His counsellor?" "Who has ever given to God, that God should repay him?" For from him and through him and to him are all things. To him be the glory for ever! Amen' (Romans 11:33–36).

Second, although we get perplexed and baffled at times at the way God works in the world, it ought never to cause us to despair. This perhaps is what Job was in danger of doing, although he did not give in to it entirely. It is not the perplexity itself that is wrong, but the sense of hopelessness it engenders and the feeling that God does not know what he is doing. Paul himself was perplexed at times by certain things in the Christian life, but he never felt things had got out of control. 'We are hard pressed on every side, but not crushed; perplexed, but not in despair' (2 Corinthians 4:8). For there is no doubt that Satan will exploit our perplexity if we let him, so that it will cause us to despair. He will whisper in our ear, 'God is not being fair with you. Here you are striving to be faithful in holy things, and all you get is trouble; whereas those who show nothing but contempt for God seem to get away with it, and everything is fine with them. Ask yourself, Is it worth it, and where does it get you in the end—this business of being God-fearing, honest and truthful?' That is the danger we must guard against, the exploitation of our perplexity by Satan, and we can best do so by adopting the principle, where God's ways are concerned, of accepting what we do not understand.

Chapter 17

Third, we must allow God to be truly God, and not some kind of cut-down version or projection of our own thinking. We must stop thinking that God should fit in with the way we want things done in this life. We can be certain that even if we are perplexed with the way things are going, God is not; he knows exactly what he is doing. And to help us think in that way we have only to remind ourselves that the doctrine of retribution of the ungodly is taught all through the Bible, along with the blessedness and reward of the godly. In the Old Testament it is summed up in the first Psalm: 'For the Lord watches over the way of the righteous, but the way of the wicked will perish' (Psalm 1:6). In the New Testament it is spelled out clearly by our Lord himself: 'Enter through the narrow gate. For wide is the gate and broad is the road that leads to destruction, and many enter through it. But small is the gate and narrow the road that leads to life, and only a few find it' (Matthew 7:13–14). So let us leave the whole matter in God's hands, knowing that as judge of all the earth he will always do what is right.

Chapter 18

A bleak view of God

Read Job chapter 22

In this, his third speech against Job, Eliphaz presents a view of God that is a mixture of truth and error. 'Then Eliphaz the Temanite replied: "Can a man be of benefit to God? Can even a wise man benefit him? What pleasure would it give the Almighty if you were righteous? What would he gain if your ways were blameless? Is it for your piety that he rebukes you and brings charges against you? Is not your wickedness great? Are not your sins endless?"' (Job 22:1–5).

God's indifference to us

Eliphaz poses a whole series of questions concerning the character and being of God, but they all relate to one thing—God's indifference both to Job and to mankind in general. Because God is all-sufficient in himself, there is nothing we can do that can benefit him or add to him in any way. He derives no pleasure from our righteousness or holiness of life; if he takes notice of us at all, it is only when we are wicked and sinful, and he then rebukes us in his wrath. Eliphaz maintains that the only reason God is showing any interest in Job is not because of his piety, but because of his wickedness. 'Is it for your piety that he rebukes you and brings charges against you? Is not your wickedness great? Are not your sins endless?' That is certainly not true of Job, as we have clearly seen.

There is, of course, more than a grain of truth in what Eliphaz is saying but, taken as a whole, he is presenting us with a pretty bleak picture of God. It is true that in our feebleness and littleness we cannot be of profit to God, as if he needed us in any way. But we dare not move on from there to the idea that he is not interested in our welfare, for then we are left with a God who is so remote and transcendent that we can have no personal relationship with him. And there are a good many sincere folk in that position in the Church today. They believe in God, maintain religious practices, share in worship and participate in the sacraments, but somehow it is all strangely impersonal and irrelevant and makes no great difference to their daily lives.

Chapter 18

But that is not how it should be. In daily life we live in close personal relationships with other people whose existence affects our own. The husband affects the wife he loves, and wife the husband; the child affects the parent and the parent the child, and so on. The question is, Can it be like that with God and ourselves?

Eliphaz seems to be saying it cannot be, because God is not sufficiently interested in us. He stands aloof from us and from the world he made. At the dawn of creation he introduced the laws necessary for its existence, and since then has allowed it to continue in its own way without any control or direction on his part. But Eliphaz is wrong in this. God is deeply interested in his children and is concerned for our welfare in this life. What happens to us matters to him. Again and again the Bible tells us that God, as a loving Father, helps us bear our burdens, calms us in our fears, guards us in times of danger, and seeks to unify our lives around his own single purpose for mankind. And, by the way we respond in obedience to this activity of God in our lives, we can bring joy and pleasure to his heart. 'For the Lord takes delight in his people; he crowns the humble with salvation' (Psalm 149:4). This personal concern of God for his people is the basic theme of the New Testament and lies at the heart of the doctrine of the Incarnation. The great awe-inspiring truth of the gospel is that, in Christ, we sinful people—through repentance and faith—can enlarge and extend our poor limited personalities by the indwelling of God himself. John puts it like this: 'We know that we live in him and he in us, because he has given us of his Spirit. And we have seen and testify that the Father has sent his Son to be the Saviour of the world. If anyone acknowledges that Jesus is the Son of God, God lives in him and he in God. And so we know and rely on the love God has for us' (1 John 4:13–16).

A charge of hypocrisy

There are few things more hurtful for the believer in this life than to have our spirituality called into question by those who claim to be our friends, and with whom we share in the things of God. Eliphaz was well aware of Job's spiritual integrity, for at the beginning of the book he commended him for it: 'Think how you have instructed many, how you have strengthened feeble hands. Your words have supported those who

A bleak view of God

stumbled; you have strengthened faltering knees' (Job 4:3–4). But now in the next section of our chapter he says, in effect, that Job is no more than a hypocrite, and all his godliness and piety a sham. He falsely accuses him of a whole catalogue of social sins against the poor and needy, the widows and fatherless: 'You demanded security from your brothers for no reason; you stripped men of their clothing, leaving them naked. You gave no water to the weary and you withheld food from the hungry, though you were a powerful man, owning land—an honoured man, living on it. And you sent widows away empty-handed and broke the strength of the fatherless' (Job 22:6–9). And, in conclusion, he tells Job that his present distress and suffering are the result of his hypocrisy and wickedness: 'That is why snares are all around you, why sudden peril terrifies you, why it is so dark that you cannot see, and why a flood of water covers you' (Job 22:10–11).

It is all a tissue of lies, as Job was quick to point out later. 'Whoever heard of me spoke well of me, and those who saw me commended me, because I rescued the poor who cried for help, and the fatherless who had none to assist him … I was eyes to the blind and feet to the lame. I was a father to the needy; I took up the case of the stranger' (Job 29:11–16). But the falseness of the charge, coming as it did from a friend, is what made it so despicable and hurtful. The believer knows he may expect that kind of thing from the world, as our Lord himself warns us: 'Blessed are you when people insult you, persecute you and falsely say all kinds of evil against you because of me' (Matthew 5:11). Such hatred is a part of the Christian warfare. But why do Christians prompt this kind of hostile reaction? The reason must be because they introduce a new and different element into any situation, so that the contrast is immediately seen and felt between the life of godliness and the life of the world. Believers bring into the environment a different set of values, and this disturbs the consciences of those around them, making them feel uncomfortable and resentful. It is not so much what the Christian says as the fact that his or her life reveals a kind of life so different from their own that it arouses hostility. To a much greater degree this was true of the Lord Jesus. When he came into the presence of evil spirits, even before he uttered a word they cried out, 'What do you want with us, Jesus of Nazareth? Have you come to destroy us? I know who you are—the Holy One of God!' (Mark 1:24).

Chapter 18

And what should be our response when people are hostile to us in this way? In the passage from Matthew quoted above, our Lord says we are to 'Rejoice and be glad, because great is your reward in heaven, for in the same way they persecuted the prophets who were before you' (Matthew 5:12). Such scorn and disapproval are themselves an evidence of the genuineness of our faith, showing that we are in line with God's servants the prophets through the ages. Furthermore, when we bear such ignominy for Christ we are laying up treasure in heaven, the reward of God's grace that we shall enter into one day.

God knows everything

Eliphaz has not finished with Job yet. He continues his attack upon his piety by accusing him of insolence towards God in saying that he does not know or see what is happening here below. 'Is not God in the heights of heaven? And see how lofty are the highest stars! Yet you say, "What does God know? Does he judge through such darkness? Thick clouds veil him, so he does not see us as he goes about in the vaulted heavens." Will you keep to the old path that evil men have trod? They were carried off before their time, their foundations washed away by a flood. They said to God, "Leave us alone! What can the Almighty do to us?"' (Job 22:12–17).

Eliphaz is saying that Job is like all the wicked people of the past, who showed contempt for God in thinking that he is out of touch with the world. He is busy in the vaulted heavens hidden by thick clouds and darkness and does not see the wickedness going on in the world. Eliphaz is wrong to apply this to Job, but what he says of man's attitude is right in principle. That is exactly how the secular man thinks of God. He may believe in a vague way that God exists, but to all intents and purposes he is a practical atheist, in the sense that he lives and behaves as if there were no God who is concerned with the moral supervision of the world. But he is a fool to think like that. God is not indifferent to sin and moral wrongdoing, and the vicious putrid things in our lives do not escape his all-seeing eye. He knows everything and sees everything, else he would not be the mighty sovereign God the Bible says he is. The Psalmist puts it so well: 'O Lord, you have searched me and you know me. You know when I sit and when I rise; you perceive my thoughts from afar. You discern my going out and my lying down; you are familiar with all my ways' (Psalm 139:1–3).

This thought that God knows everything about us is both frightening and comforting. But it is frightening only if we have something to hide. I am reminded of those people who get terribly angry about the policy of placing surveillance cameras in our towns and cities as a deterrent to crime. They say it is an affront to civil liberty. But why should anyone be afraid of being watched when he is going about his lawful business in a public place? It is like that with God and us. If we are at peace with him and know his forgiveness in Christ, then it ought not to fill us with dread that he knows all about us. Moreover, it is a comfort to know that God not only knows the ugly things that spoil and mar our lives, but also the lovely things that enhance our Christian character.

Making peace with God

Eliphaz is something of a paradox. On the one hand, he can say the most disgraceful things, even telling deliberate lies about Job. And at times, also, he has presented God as hard and vindictive, making no allowances for man's fallen nature. But then at other times, as in this final passage, he can be very tender towards Job and portrays God as loving and gracious to those who turn to him in humble repentance.

Submit to God and be at peace with him; in this way prosperity will come to you. Accept instruction from his mouth and lay up his words in your heart. If you return to the Almighty, you will be restored: if you remove wickedness far from your tent and assign your nuggets to the dust, your gold of Ophir to the rocks in the ravines, then the Almighty will be your gold, the choicest silver for you. Surely then you will find delight in the Almighty and will lift up your face to God. You will pray to him, and he will hear you, and you will fulfil your vows. What you decide on will be done, and light will shine on your ways. When men are brought low and you say, 'Lift them up!' then he will save the downcast. He will deliver even one who is not innocent, who will be delivered through the cleanness of your hands (Job 22:21–30).

Eliphaz is genuinely concerned about Job's spiritual welfare and wants him to be at peace with God. But he cannot rid himself of the idea that Job is a very wicked man who is more concerned with regaining his silver and gold

Chapter 18

than with the souls of others (Job 22:30). But although it does not fit Job's case, what he says is perfectly true. To be at peace with God is the greatest of all treasures—'the Almighty will be your gold, the choicest silver for you.' This is a wonderful expression, for it tells us that the most precious blessings of life can only become ours when we are at peace with God, when we are reconciled to him and our conscience is at rest. That is the very heart of the gospel message. 'Therefore, since we have been justified through faith, we have peace with God through our Lord Jesus Christ' (Romans 5:1). It is not just 'peace' we are offered—some kind of therapy for frayed nerves—but 'peace with God', which is much more important, for it is with God that we all have to settle accounts at the judgement.

Chapter 19

The God who hides

Read Job chapters 23 and 24

In these two chapters Job gives vent once again to his deep feelings of bitterness and sense of injustice where God is concerned. 'Then Job replied: "Even today my complaint is bitter; his hand is heavy in spite of my groaning"' (Job 23:1–2). We sometimes speak of the Lord's hand being upon us as an expression of his blessing in our lives, and that we are in the way of his will and purpose. But God's hand can be on us in another way, as when he is displeased with us or we feel that we are under his judgement. It is in that sense that Job says 'his hand is heavy' or, as we might say, 'he is being heavy-handed'. It was bad enough that his friends treated him so shabbily, but that God should treat him in such a heavy-handed way fills him with real inward pain and bewilderment. He longs to talk with God and bring his complaint before him, but when he reaches out he feels that God is not there any more. 'If only I knew where to find him; if only I could go to his dwelling! I would state my case before him and fill my mouth with arguments. I would find out what he would answer me, and consider what he would say. Would he oppose me with great power? No, he would not press charges against me. There an upright man could present his case before him, and I would be delivered for ever from my judge' (Job 23:3–7).

Where has God gone?

I remember some years ago a colleague in the ministry telling me of his experience as a boy of fifteen when his father died. He felt so lonely and miserable and wondered if God cared about him at all. One day he climbed the mountain close to his home and gave vent to his misery by looking up to the sky and shouting at the top of his voice: 'Is anyone there?' That was exactly how Job felt when in his misery he cried out in desperation, 'If only I knew where to find him'. And many of us have felt like that when we have passed through some dark experience in our lives. The world has seemed a cold and lonely place, and even God is not to be found in it. With a sense of

Chapter 19

frightened bewilderment we have said in effect, 'Where has God gone? Is he playing some cruel cosmic game of hide and seek?' Or, in Job's words: 'But if I go to the east, he is not there; if I go to the west, I do not find him. When he is at work in the north, I do not see him; when he turns to the south, I catch no glimpse of him' (Job 23:8–9).

And we are not alone in feeling this way at times. The people of the Bible had the same agonising experience that God was not there, that he had hidden himself from them. The Psalmist cried: 'Why, O Lord, do you stand far off? Why do you hide yourself in times of trouble?' (Psalm 10:1). Isaiah makes the emphatic declaration: 'Truly you are a God who hides himself, O God and Saviour of Israel' (Isaiah 45:15). During the course of the Reformation, Luther in moments of deep depression would speak of God as the Deus Absconditus (the hidden God).

But are there any reasons why God should allow us to feel that he has hidden himself from us? I believe there are.

To strengthen our faith

Sometimes God deliberately hides himself from us in order to test and strengthen our faith in him. Job is slowly coming to the realisation that that is one explanation for his own suffering. 'But he knows the way that I take; when he has tested me, I shall come forth as gold. My feet have closely followed his steps ... I have not departed from the commands of his lips; I have treasured the words of his mouth more than my daily bread' (Job 23:10,12). Peter may have had Job's experience in mind when writing, 'though now for a little while you may have had to suffer grief in all kinds of trials. These have come so that your faith—of greater worth than gold, which perishes even though refined by fire—may be proved genuine' (1 Peter 1:6–7). This refining process whereby faith is strengthened is sometimes best accomplished when all the props and supports of life are taken away from us, even the seeming withdrawal of God himself, and we only have naked faith to go on. Job is convinced he will come through this testing experience with a stronger faith, even though God has not yet finished with him. 'But he stands alone, and who can oppose him? He does whatever he pleases, he carries out his decree against me, and many such plans he still has in store. That is why I am terrified before him; when I think of all this, I fear him. God has made my heart faint; the Almighty has terrified me. Yet I am not silenced by the darkness, by the thick darkness that covers my face' (Job 23:13–17). He still feels alone and fearful and out of touch with God, yet at the same time he is certain that even the darkness and gloom of his present situation are part of God's plan for him.

Taking God for granted

Then again God can hide himself from us because of our own sin and disobedience. In this way he teaches us not to take him for granted, for we can be guilty of that. Our Christian life becomes threadbare and empty, and suddenly we find ourselves in a crisis and cry out to God for help, only to find he is not there. We sometimes treat loved ones in the same way. For years Mum is taken for granted in the home, and then suddenly she is rushed into hospital and the family feel lost and bewildered because she is no longer around. But God wants us to know we cannot treat him like that. He is not a God for the 'critical' moments only, but he wants our daily devotion.

God's non-intervention

As we move into chapter 24 Job still has a rankling sense of injustice, not this time with his own treatment but with the injustice in the world.

Why does the Almighty not set times for judgement? Why must those who know him look in vain for such days? Men move boundary stones; they pasture flocks they have stolen. They drive away the orphan's donkey and take the widow's ox in pledge. They thrust the needy from the path and force all the poor of the land into hiding. Like wild donkeys in the desert, the poor go about their labour of foraging food; the wasteland provides food for their children. They gather fodder in the fields and glean in the vineyards of the wicked. Lacking clothes, they spend the night naked; they have nothing to cover themselves in the cold (Job 24:1–7).

He continues in this way down to verse 12, describing the glaring inequalities and injustices of life, and he ends by saying, 'But God charges no-one with wrongdoing.'

Chapter 19

And that is his big problem. Where is God's justice in all this? Why does he not intervene and do something—sorting out the crooks, the swindlers, the tyrants and the bullies? Here is something that has vexed the spirits of godly men and women through the ages. We firmly believe, as the Bible teaches, that God is the God of justice, but when we look at the way he runs the world we sometimes feel it contradicts that truth. All too often it seems he is on the side of the big battalions, the people of vested interests who spurn morality and show nothing but contempt for the poor and downtrodden. And yet, as Job says, God does not seem to come down on them with the heavy hand of his justice—he 'charges no-one with wrongdoing'. In the light of that we can understand why, if we were to quote from the Sermon on the Mount the verse 'Blessed are the meek, for they will inherit the earth' (Matthew 5:5), the man in the street would laugh at us. 'Blessed are the meek? Inherit the earth? Don't you believe it! This is a tough old world and being meek won't get you anywhere, mate. People will only trample on you. If you want to inherit the good things of this earth you have to forget all about justice and fair play and Christian principles, and look after yourself by bulldozing your way to the top.'

But that approach to life was not open to Job and is certainly not open to the Christian, for the gospel forbids it. And for good reason—it does not work in the long run. 'God cannot be mocked. A man reaps what he sows' (Galatians 6:7). That is a principle God has woven into the structure of life itself. And a day will come when he will intervene, once for all, in terrible judgement. That is the conclusion Job comes to in the final section, verses 13–25. 'There are those who rebel against the light, who do not know its ways or stay in its paths' (Job 24:13). He picks out the murderer (verse 14), the adulterer (verse 15) and the robber (verse 16) as illustrating those who rebel against the light, and upon whom God's judgement will come. 'But God drags away the mighty by his power ... He may let them rest in a feeling of security, but his eyes are on their ways ... they are brought low and gathered up like all others; they are cut off like heads of grain' (Job 24:22–24). Harry Kemp, a modern American poet, has encapsulated in verse this great truth, that it is not the way of the aggressor that brings triumph and victory in the last resort, but the way of God's truth and righteousness in the Lord Jesus Christ.

The God who hides

I saw the Conquerors riding by
  with cruel lips and faces wan.
Musing on kingdoms sacked and burned
  there rode the Mongol Genghis Khan.

And Alexander like a god who sought
  to weld the world in one.
And Caesar with his laurel wreath;
  and like a thing from Hell, Attila the Hun.

And leading, like a star, the van,
  heedless of upstretched arm and groan,
Inscrutable Napoleon went dreaming
  of empire, and all alone.

Then, all they perished from the earth
  as fleeting shadows from a glass.
And conquering down the centuries
  came Christ, the swordless,
Whose Word will never pass.

Chapter 20

God's greatness, man's littleness

Read Job chapters 25 and 26

These two chapters go together because the one is the reply to the other. Chapter 25 is a mere six verses, in which Bildad makes the last of the speeches by Job's friends. He adds nothing new to what had been said earlier, but he seems anxious to impress upon Job the power and greatness of God on the one hand, and the weakness and worthlessness of man on the other. 'Then Bildad the Shuhite replied: Dominion and awe belong the God; he establishes order in the heights of heaven. Can his forces be numbered? Upon whom does his light not rise? How then can a man be righteous before God? How can one born of woman be pure? If even the moon is not bright and the stars are not pure in his eyes, how much less man, who is but a maggot—a son of man, who is only a worm!' (Job 25:2–6). In describing man as a 'maggot' and a 'worm', Bildad may have been trying to get Job to see his own worthlessness and sin and the futility of entering into controversy with God. But, whatever his motives, he is certainly telling us something we need to be reminded of where God is concerned.

Mighty God
The doctrine concerning the greatness and power of God is one that needs to be rediscovered and revitalised in the Church today, and especially in the pulpit. All too often God is presented as though he were not that different from ourselves, a kind of superman rather than the mighty God. So much of the majesty and awe attaching to God's being, which is portrayed so powerfully in the Bible, is missing from today's worship services. We do not have to go all the way with the theology of Karl Barth to appreciate his emphasis upon God as the 'wholly other', for that is what is lacking in today's understanding of God. There are some very fine modern hymns and choruses being written today for use in worship, but all too often they

God's greatness, man's littleness

fail to project God in this awesome way. Bildad captures something of the grandeur of God's administration when, referring to the angelic powers at God's command, he asks, 'Can his forces be numbered?' This puts us in mind of the words of Jesus: 'Do you think I cannot call on my Father, and he will at once put at my disposal more than twelve legions of angels?' (Matthew 26:3). He asks further: 'Upon whom does his light not rise?' indicating that God's dominion and providential care extend to all men everywhere, and all are dependent on him.

The failure to give due emphasis to God's majesty and power in our worship and preaching has had serious consequences for the Church's witness. Men and women no longer have the fear of God in their hearts; sin has lost its character as a radical alienation from God, and there is no longer that sense of accountability before the bar of God's judgement. Another consequence has been that Christians themselves have lost heart in the struggle of life. Because their concept of God is small and meagre, their faith has became soft and flabby and unequal to the pressures and tensions we are all subject to in today's world. They feel within themselves that God has somehow lost his grip on things and that he is as mixed up and confused about life as they are. That is a great pity, because it means that they are living at a sub-Christian level, in the flats and shallows instead of being borne along on the wave of God's grace and keeping power.

Little man

With Job still in mind, Bildad turns his attention to the depravity and worthlessness of man. 'How then can a man be righteous before God? How can one born of woman be pure? If even the moon is not bright and the stars are not pure in his eyes, how much less man, who is but a maggot—a son of man who is only a worm!' (Job 25:4–6). Many would find this description deeply offensive and very demeaning of our humanity. But the Bible is in absolute agreement with Bildad, for he is describing the weakness and corruptibility of our human nature. And who can deny that? The evidences of the corrosive effects of sin in the human heart are all around us. We read about them every day in the newspapers, or hear them reported on the television.

It is in the light of this human condition that Bildad asks, 'How then can

Chapter 20

a man be righteous before God? How can one born of woman be pure?' Man cannot contribute in any way to his own salvation. His depravity is total—not in the sense that he is incapable of doing anything good, but in the sense that sin has tainted every part of his nature. The totality of his being is affected by sin: his heart, will, conscience, intellect and everything else. This doctrine of man's total depravity is clearly taught in Scripture: 'Never again will I curse the ground because of man, even though every inclination of his heart is evil from childhood' (Genesis 8:21); 'Surely I was sinful at birth, sinful from the time my mother conceived me' (Psalm 51:5); 'All of us also lived ... gratifying the cravings of our sinful nature and following its desires and thoughts. Like the rest, we were by nature objects of wrath' (Ephesians 2:3). Clearly man's natural condition is one of total inability to procure his own salvation.

One other passage of Scripture where man's corruptibility is symbolised by the worm is Psalm 22. 'But I am a worm and not a man, scorned by men and despised by the people. All who see me mock me; they hurl insults, shaking their heads: "He trusts in the Lord; let the Lord rescue him. Let him deliver him, since he delights in him"' (Psalm 22:6–8). What makes these words significant is that they appear in what is regarded as a Messianic psalm, and are prophetic of Christ as our sin-bearer taking our corruptibility on himself. 'God made him who had no sin to be sin for us, so that in him we might become the righteousness of God' (2 Corinthians 5:21). Salvation by its very nature is something only God himself can give us.

In chapter 26 Job replies to Bildad, and he does so with biting sarcasm. 'Then Job replied: "How you have helped the powerless! How you have saved the arm that is feeble! What advice you have offered to one without wisdom! And what great insight you have displayed! Who has helped you utter these words? And whose spirit spoke from your mouth?"' (Job 26:1–4). It is as if he were saying: 'Oh, you are a great help, you are, Bildad! Here am I, in all kinds of mental and physical distress, and all you can do is preach to me about the majesty of God and the worthlessness of man! I know all that already. What kind of advice is it to a man in my predicament to be told that he is a worm in God's sight? All that you've said about God and man is perfectly true but totally irrelevant in my case. It doesn't help me one little bit.'

Applying the Word

As far as Job was concerned Bildad was preaching an old sermon. He was like an old gramophone record being played over again and again. It was not that what he said was untrue, or that Job did not agree with him, but that it had no personal application in Job's situation. Does that say something to us as preachers? Biblical preaching is applicatory preaching; it brings the great truths and principles of Scripture to bear upon people's lives just where they are, with all their trials and difficulties. The preacher must remind himself of that fact. He is not in the pulpit to deliver a theological lecture, or to relate some interesting anecdotes, or to offer a few moral platitudes. He is dealing with real people, living in the real world, who need to know what God has to say to them that will enable them to handle their own personal life situations.

The relevance of the message will differ with different people. They will be helped or encouraged, or made aware of their sins, or made to realise the poor quality of their spiritual lives, or made resentful even; but if it is the Word of God they will not go away chatting amiably as if the whole thing were a non-event. Furthermore, the failure of the message to have personal application may not be the fault of the preacher but of the listener. What is our state of mind in attending a service of worship? Are we there to sing some favourite hymns, to meet socially and to hear a man air his personal opinions for putting the world to rights? Or are we there in a humble spirit to meet with the living God and to hear what he has to say to us out of his Word?

The fringe of God's ways

As if to impress upon Bildad his own belief in the greatness and awesomeness of God, Job proceeds to speak of God's power in creation, doing so in language of great poetic beauty: 'The dead are in deep anguish, those beneath the waters and all that live in them. Death is naked before God; Destruction lies uncovered' (Job 26:5–6). 'Job rivals Bildad in magnifying the greatness of God', comments A. B. Davidson. He begins with his omnipresence: God is everywhere; his immensity permeates even down to Sheol, the abode of the dead and of evil spirits. It is the thought of Psalm 139: 'Where can I go from your Spirit? Where can I flee from your

Chapter 20

presence? If I go up to the heavens, you are there; if I make my bed in the depths, you are there' (Psalm 139:7-8). The same thought is repeated in Philippians 2: 'that at the name of Jesus every knee should bow, in heaven and on earth and under the earth' (Philippians 2:10).

From under the earth, Job moves to God's power at work in the heavens. 'He spreads out the northern skies over empty space; he suspends the earth over nothing. He wraps up the waters in his clouds, yet the clouds do not burst under their weight. He covers the face of the full moon, spreading his clouds over it' (Job 26:7-9). He then traces God's handiwork in the realm of nature. 'He marks out the horizon on the face of the waters for a boundary between light and darkness. The pillars of the heavens quake, aghast at his rebuke' (Job 26:10-11). By 'pillars' is meant poetically the mountains, and their 'quaking' is the effect of earthquakes or volcanoes. 'By his power he churned up the sea; by his wisdom he cut Rahab to pieces' (Job 26:12). This may be a reference not only to God's power in the storm, but also to his mighty miracle in dividing the waters at the Red Sea and the destruction of the Egyptian Pharaoh—'Rahab' being the symbolic name for ancient Egypt (Isaiah 30:7). Job continues: 'By his breath the skies became fair; his hand pierced the gliding serpent' (Job 26:13). God's power in the control over the forces of nature is seen equally in the quiet and calm after the storm when the skies become bright and fair, and even extends beyond the physical creation to the moral and spiritual realm where his hand 'pierced the gliding serpent'. This again is an Old Testament symbol for the heathen powers and the forces of evil (Isaiah 27:1). One of the many names given to Satan in the Bible is 'serpent', and Job is indicating in this poetic fashion the triumph of divine power over the forces of darkness.

The poem comes to its conclusion with these remarkable words: 'And these are but the outer fringe of his works; how faint the whisper we hear of him! Who then can understand the thunder of his power?' (Job 26:14). All the mighty miracles and manifestations of power we witness in the realm of creation are in the end only the 'fringe', a tiny 'glimpse' of God's greatness, a mere 'whisper', as it were, of his activity. If then it is so difficult to understand and comprehend the little that we know about God, says Job, what hope have we of ever grasping the fullness or 'thunder' of his sovereign might?

And he is absolutely right. We can never hope fully to comprehend God. That is something that still awaits us in the future: 'Now I know in part; then I shall know fully, even as I am fully known' (1 Corinthians 13:12). But we must also keep in mind that Job was speaking at a time in history before the fullness of God's revelation in Christ. In the realm of saving grace we have indeed experienced the fullness of divine power. 'For God was pleased to have all his fulness dwell in him, and through him to reconcile to himself all things, whether things on earth or things in heaven, by making peace through his blood, shed on the cross' (Colossians 1:19). How blessed and privileged we are therefore to live on this side of Calvary!

Chapter 21

Job's integrity

Read Job chapter 27

The opening verses of this chapter reveal the turbulent state of mind to which Job's sufferings had brought him. He begins with a solemn oath. 'And Job continued his discourse: "As surely as God lives, who has denied me justice, the Almighty, who has made me taste bitterness of soul"' (Job 27:1–2).

The fire of conviction

On the one hand, he is calling upon the living God to be a witness to the truth of what he is about to say: on the other hand, it is the same living God he is about to accuse of denying him justice and causing him bitterness of soul. It is as if there were two conceptions of God struggling for mastery within him. But although his emotions are in turmoil, and his mind baffled and bewildered by what is happening to him, we get the feeling that here is a man speaking with the fire of conviction concerning his own spiritual integrity and faith. God is still the living God in whom he trusts and to whom he appeals to solve his dilemma.

We are living at a time when people seem to lack deep convictions about anything, whether in political and social ideals or the truths of religion. For the most part they seem, in our society at least, to be absorbed only with their own pleasures and prosperity. Leisure is a growth industry in our country: the holiday trade is booming, and sport is a multimillion-pound business with hundreds of thousands of followers for whom it is the central feature of their lives. The fashion industry is equally prosperous and buoyant; on a television programme recently we were told that men's interest in the use of cosmetics now involved a staggering turnover of three hundred million pounds a year, and was growing fast. It all seems, on reflection, to be a sad commentary on the emptiness and vanity of people's lives in an age that has lost any deeply rooted beliefs or convictions in the things of the spirit.

And it has to be admitted that this flabbiness of thinking has infected the very soul of the Church, so that many Christians are facing a real crisis of faith and confidence. All the week Christians are having to rub shoulders with secularly minded people in shops and offices and schools and factories, and are subject to pressures that undermine spiritual values and obliterate the distinction between themselves and that worldly environment. And because they do not have the depth of conviction to rise to the challenge, they drift into an acceptance of that environment and take on board many of its worse features. Many fail, I believe, not because they do not try, but because they are not making use of the right resources. Paul deals with this very subject in his letter to the Corinthians. 'For no-one can lay any foundation other than the one already laid, which is Jesus Christ. If any man builds on this foundation using gold, silver, costly stones, wood, hay or straw, his work will be shown for what it is, because the Day will bring it to light' (1 Corinthians 3:11–12). The distinction is between resources or materials that are strong and durable, and those that are shoddy and perishable. A strong Christian character and lasting convictions are built with the sound teaching of God's Word and prayer, not with the flimsy values of our consumer society.

Spiritual integrity

Job's strong sense of conviction is given further expression as he defends his innocence before the accusations of his friends: 'as long as I have life within me, the breath of God in my nostrils, my lips will not speak wickedness, and my tongue will utter no deceit. I will never admit you are in the right; till I die, I will not deny my integrity. I will maintain my righteousness and never let go of it; my conscience will not reproach me as long as I live' (Job 27: 3–6). He is inwardly confident of his moral and spiritual integrity, and he had every right to be so, since God himself had made that the battleground for the conflict with Satan at the outset of the book. 'Then the Lord said to Satan, "Have you considered my servant Job? There is no-one on earth like him; he is blameless and upright, a man who fears God and shuns evil. And he still maintains his integrity, though you incited me against him to ruin him without any reason"' (Job 2:3). As Job sees it, to deny his integrity in the face of his friends' accusations would be to deny God and undermine the very foundation of his faith. In relation to his

Chapter 21

integrity he mentions two very important things: the need for truth and a quiet conscience.

Speaking the truth

Job vows, 'my lips will not speak wickedness, and my tongue will utter no deceit' (Job 27:4). There is such a thing as the integrity of language, and when earlier Job had sworn a solemn oath, 'As surely as God lives', that is what he had in mind. Under the Old Testament dispensation God's law on oath-taking was intended to guard the solemnity of the truth. 'When a man makes a vow to the Lord or takes an oath to bind himself by a pledge, he must not break his word but must do everything he said' (Numbers 30:2). To take an oath was to invoke God's involvement as a witness to the truth.

In the light of this we can now understand the significance of our Lord's words: 'Again, you have heard that it was said to the people long ago, "Do not break your oath, but keep the oaths you have made to the Lord" … But I tell you, do not swear at all: either by heaven, for it is God's throne; or by the earth, for it is his footstool; or by Jerusalem, for it is the city of the Great King. And do not swear by your head, for you cannot make even one hair white or black. Simply let your 'Yes' be 'Yes' and your 'No', 'No'; anything beyond this comes from the evil one' (Matthew 5:33–37). By our Lord's time there was a good deal of flippancy in the matter of oath-taking and men would swear by anything; but Jesus is warning them that this is to trivialise the truth. Far better not to swear oaths at all, but simply to say what we mean, and mean what we say—to let our 'Yes' be 'Yes' and our 'No' be 'No'.

In the Christian life there is no place for the kind of double-talk we hear so much of today. We are all well acquainted with the 'credibility gap' in public and political life, when politicians say one thing but mean something else. There is so much of this falsity and deception in modern life, where truth no longer seems to matter, where vows and promises in personal relationships are easily broken, and agreements in business and management often disregarded. It all makes for growing tension and distrust, and that cannot help to promote a happy and contented society. When a Christian says 'Yes' or 'No', therefore, he must mean it and have no need of any oath to back up the truth of what he says. It all comes down in the end to spiritual integrity: 'Since we live by the Spirit, let us keep in step with the Spirit' (Galatians 5:25).

A quiet conscience

'I will maintain my righteousness and never let go of it; my conscience will not reproach me as long as I live' (Job 27:6). By his righteousness he means his inward integrity before God, and therefore his conscience is at perfect peace with regard to the sins his friends have accused him of.

The New Testament has a great deal to say about conscience. To begin with, everybody has one; it is a part of the moral equipment God designed us with at birth. Paul says we can appeal to a person's conscience when we present them with the truth of the Gospel: 'by setting forth the truth plainly we commend ourselves to every man's conscience in the sight of God' (2 Corinthians 4:2). As a warning system within our moral framework, conscience is so important that people who have never heard the gospel will finally be judged by God according to how they have obeyed its dictates in this life: '(Indeed, when Gentiles, who do not have the law, do by nature things required by the law, they are a law for themselves ... their consciences also bearing witness, and their thoughts now accusing, now even defending them.) This will take place on the day when God will judge men's secrets through Jesus Christ' (Romans 2:14–16).

The conscience, however, is not an infallible guide to moral behaviour, because we can choose to suppress the feelings of guilt it arouses in us when we do something wrong. And if we neglect its warning signals often enough, it can lose its sensitivity and become totally unreliable. Like a watch or car, or any other piece of equipment we use in everyday life, the conscience needs to be serviced and cared for if it is to function reliably. We do this through the regular discipline of prayer and worship, and by exposing it to the cutting edge of God's Word.

The fate of the wicked

There is not much we need to say about the remaining section of this chapter (from verse 7 following), because it contains yet another poem on the fate of the wicked. This is a familiar theme in the book and has been well covered in chapters 15, 18 and 20. Job begins with what seems like a

Chapter 21

curse or imprecation upon the friends Eliphaz, Bildad and Zophar who had been so hostile towards him: 'May my enemies be like the wicked, my adversaries like the unjust! For what hope has the godless when he is cut off, when God takes away his life? Does God listen to his cry when distress comes upon him? Will he find delight in the Almighty? Will he call upon God at all times?' (Job 27:7–10).

If he did have his friends in mind, Job was not being merely vindictive or malicious. This is clear when he says later that he has not 'rejoiced at my enemy's misfortune or gloated over the trouble that came to him—I have not allowed my mouth to sin by invoking a curse against his life' (Job 31:29–30). His chief motive therefore is the vindication of God's truth, and the desire that spiritual integrity should be seen to triumph over wickedness and the powers of evil in the world.

Chapter 22

The nature of wisdom

Read Job chapter 28

The passage we are now considering stands in direct contrast to all the inner wrestling and heated words we have encountered in many of the previous chapters. What we have here is a quiet, serene meditation by Job on the meaning of wisdom. It seems he has reached a point where he realises that all the arguments he and his friends have put forward to try and explain God's dealings with him have been futile, because there is so much about God that is incomprehensible to us with our limited knowledge. What is needed is true wisdom. But where can it be found? That is the question Job seeks to answer.

Human knowledge

He begins with a vivid and fascinating description of man's skill and knowledge as applied to ancient mining techniques for getting out the riches of the earth.

There is a mine for silver and a place where gold is refined. Iron is taken from the earth, and copper is smelted from ore. Man puts an end to the darkness; he searches the farthest recesses for ore in the blackest darkness. Far from where people dwell he cuts a shaft, in places forgotten by the foot of man; far from men he dangles and sways. The earth, from which food comes, is transformed below as by fire; sapphires come from its rocks, and its dust contains nuggets of gold. No bird of prey knows that hidden path, no falcon's eye has seen it. Proud beasts do not set foot on it, and no lion prowls there. Man's hand assaults the flinty rock and lays bare the roots of the mountains. He tunnels through the rock; his eyes see all its treasures. He searches the sources of the rivers and brings hidden things to light (Job 28:1–11).

That is a wonderful poetic description, extolling the knowledge and technical genius which make man superior to all the other creatures. And when we reflect on the tremendous advances man has made since that time—in the understanding of his natural environment; in medical science,

From despair to hope 131

Chapter 22

enabling people to live longer and healthier lives; in the field of transport, enabling us to get to our destination faster and in greater comfort; and in the provision of better housing, with all the labour-saving devices that make life easier and more enjoyable—we must surely be truly thankful to God. For these are all real blessings that help to enrich our lives in this world. But having acknowledged the extent and worth of human knowledge and ingenuity, Job then pauses and asks a question. 'But where can wisdom be found? Where does understanding dwell? Man does not comprehend its worth; it cannot be found in the land of the living. The deep says, "It is not in me"; the sea says, "It is not with me"' (Job 28:12–14).

Wisdom

In asking that question Job is saying two things. First, he is saying that knowledge and wisdom are not the same thing. Man has plenty of knowledge, and through his science and technology he is able to mine the treasures of the earth, plumb the depths of the oceans, send rockets into outer space, transplant human organs, send messages round the world in seconds, experiment with the human genetic structure, and do many other wonderful things. But possessing all this knowledge and cleverness does not seem to make man any wiser. If it did we should have no worries whatever about the future of our world or about the environment, because every year we spend hundreds of millions of pounds on providing better education for our children and giving them more and more knowledge. But the truth is that we are worried about the future of our world and the kind of environment we are creating. Governments are worried about the political instability of the world. Political parties worry about the state of society and the economy. Police authorities worry about rising crime. Parents worry about their children growing up in a culture of violence and drugs, and teachers and social workers worry about growing vice and immorality.

And the reason we worry is this: in spite of the millions we spend on educating our children, we know that when it comes to using that knowledge for the good of mankind, they will not necessarily be any wiser than our generation. And that is the second thing Job is saying: however great man's knowledge, without the wisdom and insight to use that

The nature of wisdom

knowledge aright it is still very limited in what it can achieve. Medical science enables us to live longer lives, but that does not mean we are living any better. Modern transport can get us to our destination a lot more quickly, but that does not mean there are better places to get to. Our houses may be of better design and more comfortable to live in, but that is not to say that they make better homes or that happier families live in them. Food technology and production produce ever-growing surpluses, but a large part of the world still goes hungry. Our understanding of human psychology is greater than ever before, and yet relationships in society are more contentious and fractured than many of us can ever remember. It seems that human knowledge has advanced tremendously in certain directions, but when it comes to the really important things, like living together in peace and harmony and creating a happier and more contented society, it has hardly advanced at all.

This is the point the apostle Paul makes when he asks, 'Where is the wise man? Where is the scholar? Where is the philosopher of this age? Has not God made foolish the wisdom [knowledge] of the world?' (1 Corinthians 1:20). He is saying in effect, 'Where has all our cleverness and knowledge got us in the end? Look at our world, the mess we have got ourselves into. Hasn't God shown what foolishness it all is?' And he is right. Man seems trapped in a web of his own making. The more he advances in knowledge, the more numerous and complex his problems become, so that the very peace and happiness he hopes his knowledge will bring elude him continually.

Wisdom is precious

Job goes on to say that wisdom is so precious a commodity that all the wealth of the world cannot purchase it. 'It cannot be bought with the finest gold, nor can its price be weighed in silver. It cannot be bought with the gold of Ophir, with precious onyx or sapphires. Neither gold nor crystal can compare with it, nor can it be had for jewels of gold. Coral and jasper are not worthy of mention; the price of wisdom is beyond rubies. The topaz of Cush cannot compare with it; it cannot be bought with pure gold' (Job 28:15–19).

Why does Job rate wisdom so highly? Because it is something we all

Chapter 22

need, and yet we have no hope of acquiring it in the way we acquire other things, because it is hidden from us and we do not even know where to start looking for it. 'Where then does wisdom come from? Where does understanding dwell? It is hidden from the eyes of every living thing, concealed even from the birds of the air. Destruction and Death say, "Only a rumour of it has reached our ears"' (Job 28:20–22). Whereas we can acquire most other things in this life with money, there is no market place where wisdom is bought and sold. Not even the most expensive education at one of our great public schools can give it to us.

God the source of wisdom

In the concluding section of the chapter, Job finally answers the question, Where can wisdom be found? 'God understands the way to it and he alone knows where it dwells, for he views the ends of the earth and sees everything under the heavens. When he established the force of the wind and measured out the waters, when he made a decree for the rain and a path for the thunderstorm, then he looked at wisdom and appraised it; he confirmed it and tested it. And he said to man, "The fear of the Lord—that is wisdom, and to shun evil is understanding"' (Job 28:23–28). He is giving us a definition of wisdom and he is telling us how we are to possess it. We have to be humble enough to come to terms with the mighty God of creation. We must bow down before him in reverence and fear, acknowledge the limitations of our humanity and of our knowledge and powers of reasoning, and be prepared to accept that there are things in this life we shall never fully understand in and of ourselves. Why am I here in this life? What is it all about? Where have I come from? And where am I going when it all ends? These are questions that are answered satisfactorily only when we humbly recognise that our times are in God's hands, and that he is the one who controls and governs all things by his power. Only then do we receive that wisdom and insight into his eternal purposes for ourselves and our world.

But there is also a practical side to wisdom that is of help to us here and now for the living of our lives in today's world. In the New Testament, James comes to the same conclusion as to the source of wisdom as Job did: 'If any of you lacks wisdom, he should ask God, who gives generously to all without finding fault; and it will be given to him' (James 1:5). In the preceding verses he has been talking about the way in which we face up to the trials and difficulties of life, and he is now saying to do that successfully we need the insight [wisdom] and discernment that come from our relationship with God in Christ. 'It is because of him that you are in Christ Jesus, who has become for us wisdom from God' (1 Corinthians 1:30). When we come to faith in Christ, he, as the wisdom of God, reveals to us the mind of God so that a new life principle enters into us. We begin to see things in God's way and are able to discern more clearly between right and wrong and to cope more efficiently with life's difficult situations.

Chapter 23

Job's golden past

Read Job chapter 29

One is almost tempted to call this chapter 'The good old days'. For here is Job meditating on his past life, his thoughts lingering wistfully on the memory of days filled with happiness and prosperity. He is led to do this because of his present predicament, and his thoughts stand in stark contrast to his sad lament in the following chapter (30) which we shall call 'Job's present misery'.

God at the centre

In the opening verses he tells us that his past happiness and blessing arose mainly from the conviction that God was watching over him. 'Job continued his discourse: "How I long for the months gone by, for the days when God watched over me, when his lamp shone upon my head and by his light I walked through darkness!"' (Job 29:1–3). Some commentators blame Job for looking back over his past life and see it as a sign that he had lost the sense of fellowship with God in his present trials. As believers, they maintain, we should forget past blessings and concentrate on going forward with Christ into the future. And to support this point of view they love to quote Paul's words: 'Forgetting what is behind and straining towards what is ahead, I press on towards the goal to win the prize for which God has called me heavenwards in Christ Jesus' (Philippians 3:13). 'There you are,' they say, 'Paul didn't glory in his past. He put it behind him, and that is what we must do.'

They seem to overlook the fact that Paul's past was totally different from Job's, and one he was glad to put behind him. He says in that same chapter (Philippians 3) that he had persecuted the Church of Christ and that the things that filled up his past life he now considered rubbish. Job, on the other hand, is looking back to his past life with gratitude and praise, for God was at the centre of his life and thinking, and in his service he had found his chief happiness and joy. God's truth had been like a lamp in the darkness, enabling him to move forward in life with confidence. God was at the centre of his

Job's golden past

home and family life. 'Oh, for the days when I was in my prime, when God's intimate friendship blessed my house, when the Almighty was still with me and my children were around me' (Job 29:4–5). He recalls the material prosperity he had enjoyed in past days, 'when my path was drenched with cream and the rock poured out for me streams of olive oil' (Job 29:6). But even his affluence he attributes to God's watchful care over him, for we know from God's own assessment of him that he never allowed his wealth and prosperity to make him proud and indifferent to God's goodness. 'Have you considered my servant Job? There is no-one on earth like him; he is blameless and upright, a man who fears God and shuns evil' (Job 1:8).

Clearly it is neither wrong nor unspiritual to look back on a past life like that, when we have known the nearness and blessedness of God's presence in a very real way. Of course we should not live in the past as some Christians do, always relating past experiences and blessings but having little to say about their relationship with God in the present. But looking back to God's goodness in the past can be a valuable exercise, and one that inspires and encourages us in the present and for the future. We have a good illustration of this from the life of Jacob. When he was dying his mind went back over his long life, and the one experience that stood out in his memory was the meeting with God at Bethel. 'God Almighty appeared to me at Bethel in the land of Canaan, and there he blessed me, and said to me, "I am going to make you fruitful … and I will give this land as an everlasting possession to your descendants after you"' (Genesis 48:3–4). That encounter with God served as an anchor for Jacob in all the troubles and trials of his future life, right up to his dying day.

We all need a Bethel, some deep awareness of the reality of God's love in Christ to which we can look back and which serves as an anchor for the soul. When we are tempted to doubt the reality of God's presence with us, we can look back, as Job does, to all those times when God was right at the centre of our lives and our hearts were warm with his presence. This encourages and fortifies us, and we can say to ourselves, 'God was real to me then. How can I ever doubt his presence with me now?'

The respect of others

In reflecting on his past life Job remembers the high esteem in which he was

Chapter 23

held in the community and the active part he played in its social and political life. 'When I went to the gate of the city and took my place in the public square, the young men saw me and stepped aside and the old men rose to their feet; the chief men refrained from speaking and covered their mouths with their hands; the voices of the nobles were hushed, and their tongues stuck to the roof of their mouths' (Job 29:7–10). The city gate was a hub of community life; it was here that social and business matters would be discussed and the elders made decisions. Job was a city elder and a member of its ruling council. He describes still further his role as a community leader: 'Men listened to me expectantly, waiting in silence for my counsel. After I had spoken, they spoke no more; my words fell gently on their ears. They waited for me as for showers and drank in my words as the spring rain. When I smiled at them, they scarcely believed it; the light of my face was precious to them. I chose the way for them and sat as their chief; I dwelt as a king among his troops; I was like one who comforts mourners' (Job 29:21–25).

One writer says of this passage, 'It is pitiful to hear a truly great man describing his supremacy over others.' And he asks, '... had not this sense of his greatness fostered a pride in Job which made his downfall a necessary dealing of God?' (Ridout, The Book of Job). I disagree most emphatically. To begin with, Job did not suffer any 'downfall'; rather it was because of his spiritual integrity and blamelessness that God chose his life as a battleground for the contest with the forces of evil. And it was not pride in his supremacy and wisdom that motivated Job to speak of the respect he commanded from others, but his certainty that God's hand of blessing was upon his life. Others recognised the mark of God upon him, and it was this that made his counsel accepted by all classes in the community and gave his civic leadership such high value.

And that surely is saying certain things to us. First, it reminds us that as God's people we must be careful to live and act in public and community life in such a way that we maintain the integrity of the gospel. Our neighbours and the people we live and work with should recognise that because we are Christian believers our word can be relied upon, that we are scrupulously honest and truthful and therefore worthy of their respect. Writing of the qualities needed in a Christian pastor Paul says: 'He must also have a good reputation with outsiders, so that he will not fall into disgrace and into the devil's trap' (1 Timothy 3:7). And in his letter to Titus Paul has something to say about Christian citizenship and service in the community. 'Remind the people to be subject to rulers and authorities, to be obedient, to be ready to do whatever is good, to slander no-one, to be peaceable and considerate, and to show true humility towards all men' (Titus 3:1–2).

Secondly, it is showing how needful and necessary it is for godly people like Job, if they have the ability and qualifications, to play an active part in the social and political life of the community. He was a city elder and magistrate and was able to have an influence on social issues and matters relating to local government. Our world today is suffering from a crisis in leadership, and it is an indication of how far we have strayed from the principles of Scripture in our own nation that we hear so much of corruption and immorality in public and political life. If we want our nation's life to be influenced by the Spirit of God, then it can only happen when more Christian men and women are prepared to enter public affairs. There are many examples given in the Bible: Joseph was Prime Minister in Egypt; Daniel was a leading statesman in the Babylonian empire, and Nehemiah was the Governor of Jerusalem. In his statement that we are to 'Give to Caesar what is Caesar's' (Matthew 22:21) our Lord was recognising the right the State has over its subjects. Paul likewise says, 'The authorities that exist have been established by God' (Romans 13:1). And even if we are not actively engaged in public affairs ourselves, we are exhorted to pray for those that are—'for kings and all those in authority, that we may live peaceful and quiet lives in all godliness and holiness' (1 Timothy 2:2).

Helping the poor and needy

The respect with which Job was held in the community was also engendered by his concern for the downtrodden.

Whoever heard me spoke well of me, and those who saw me commended me, because I rescued the poor who cried for help, and the fatherless who had none to assist him. The man who was dying blessed me; I made the widow's heart sing. I put on righteousness as

Chapter 23

my clothing; justice was my robe and my turban. I was eyes to the blind and feet to the lame. I was a father to the needy; I took up the case of the stranger. I broke the fangs of the wicked and snatched the victims from their teeth (Job 29:11–17).

What impressed people, especially the poor, was the fact that Job's deep faith in God was not divorced from the practicalities of life. It is true that he was prosperous and influential, but he used his wealth and position under God to help the widows and orphans and the powerless members in the community. Where there was oppression he used his magisterial authority to punish the oppressors and 'snatched the victims from their teeth'.

It is a shameful evidence of man's sin that in our modern world, where we have both the resources and the means to ensure that everyone can live decently and with dignity, the problems of poverty, hunger and disease are still with us on a vast scale, and even, in some areas of the world, are getting ever greater. As Christians we cannot ignore that fact. So it becomes an imperative of our faith to help those in need. We must do this both at the personal level and, by our support of missionary organisations and charitable causes, feed and clothe the poor of the world, provide medical care and, in general, ease the burdens of our common life. This is love in action, and John, in his epistle, sees it as an extension of the principle of self-sacrifice exemplified in the cross: 'This is how we know what love is: Jesus Christ laid down his life for us. And we ought to lay down our lives for our brothers. If anyone has material possessions and sees his brother in need but has no pity on him, how can the love of God be in him? Dear children, let us not love with words or tongue but with actions and in truth' (1 John 3:16–18).

Job's big mistake

Having reflected on the happiness and prosperity of his past life, Job is also honest enough to tell us that he made one big mistake. 'I thought, I shall die in my own house, my days as numerous as the grains of sand. My roots will reach to the water, and the dew will lie all night on my branches. My glory will remain fresh in me, the bow ever new in my hand' (Job 29 18–20). He deluded himself into thinking that this idyllic state of affairs would go on for ever. He envisaged future days stretching out as 'numerous as the grains

Job's golden past

of sand' and he would continue to prosper and flourish like a healthy tree with its roots in the water. But it was not to be. His dream was rudely shattered when Satan unleashed his onslaught on him. It was then that his trust in God was really put to the test.

Are we in danger of making the same mistake, and becoming too earthbound? Not that we become fixated with this life and its material blessings, any more than Job was, but somehow we fail to sit as loosely to it as we might. The truth is that nothing associated with this life lasts for ever. Yet millions live as though that were not true. I remember hearing or reading somewhere that God made man from the dust of the ground, and the way some folk hang on to it you would think it was gold dust! By all means let us enjoy the good things of this life as a gift from God, but let us also keep them in their proper place by sitting lightly to them. Our circumstances might change and we might be called to give them up. And then only God remains.

Chapter 24

Job's present misery

Read Job chapter 30

Pleasant and uplifting though it has been for Job to reflect upon the blessing and prosperity of his past life, he is forced at last to come back to the reality of the present with his opening words 'But now'. And an unhappy present it is! This is a sad, sad chapter, in which he contrasts the misery and suffering he is now experiencing with the life he once knew.

The contempt of others

In his past life Job had been accustomed to receiving the respect of others in society, but now his reputation was in tatters and he had become an object of contempt and loathing.

But now they mock me, men younger than I, whose fathers I would have disdained to put with my sheep dogs. Of what use was the strength of their hands to me, since their vigour had gone from them? Haggard from want and hunger, they roamed the parched land in desolate wastelands at night. In the brush they gathered salt herbs, and their food was the root of the broom tree. They were banished from their fellow-men, shouted at as if they were thieves ... they were driven out of the land. And now their sons mock me in song ... they do not hesitate to spit in my face. Now that God has unstrung my bow and afflicted me, they throw off restraint in my presence (Job 30:1–11).

He continues his lament in the same strain, ending with the words, 'my dignity is driven away as by the wind, my safety vanishes like a cloud' (verse 15).

All this is deeply moving and we cannot help feeling sorry for Job. Here were young men, who had themselves been driven out of decent society because of their behaviour, pouring contempt and derision on him. They were singing ribald obscene songs about him (verse 9), poking fun at his diseased and wasted body, spitting in his face and, in general, treating him like a piece of garbage. It was all so hurtful and soul-destroying. When he was prosperous and successful Job was held in high regard and esteem, but now that his wealth and position have gone he is despised. What does that teach us? It certainly tells us not to lay too much store by the praises of men and the popularity of the world. Worldly praise is an ephemeral thing; it can be here today and gone tomorrow. You have only to look at the world of show business and entertainment to see the truth of that. Those who were once the idols of an adoring public are now forgotten. And yet this desire for worldly success and the flattery and praise of others exercises an enormous influence over people's hearts and minds, even in the Christian life.

John in his Gospel gives us a good illustration of that kind of thing. 'Yet at the same time many even among the leaders believed in him. But because of the Pharisees they would not confess their faith for fear they would be put out of the synagogue; for they loved praise from men more than praise from God' (John 12:42–43). Here were men in prominent positions of leadership who had come to a measure of faith in Christ but whose pride and vanity prevented them making their convictions known. They valued the praise and good opinion of others and were afraid that if they sided with Christ they would lose all that. And this can still be a stumbling block for Christians today. The good opinion of others feeds our pride and inflates our egos and can lead us to keep quiet about our Christian convictions for fear of being laughed at and ridiculed. But how short-sighted this is—as if what others think of us is more important than what God thinks of us! The praise and flattery of the world, as in Job's case, is short-lived, whereas the praise and approbation of God are eternal.

Job's contempt

But there is something more here. Who were these people who derided Job and mocked him? They were themselves objects of contempt. They were the drop-outs of the ancient world, the equivalent of our drug addicts, alcoholics, the winos hanging around in our town parks and the inhabitants of our cardboard cities. We sense a measure of contempt on Job's part in his description of them. So low are they in his sight that he says he would not have put their fathers with his sheep dogs (Job 30:1). Dogs were looked upon as scavengers in the ancient world. When he was a great

Chapter 24

landowner he would not employ them, because they were lazy and lacked strength and vigour (Job 30:2); they were vagabonds and rabble, living by their wits and thievery (Job 30:3–5), 'a base and nameless brood' (Job 30:8). We can feel sorry for Job, but we cannot overlook the fact that there is a note of deep resentment and wounded pride in the contemptuous manner in which he speaks of these people. He has become an object of abuse and insult to those who were socially his inferiors, and he feels humiliated and robbed of his dignity as a human being: 'my dignity is driven away as by the wind (Job 30:15). We can understand all that, because it is what is happening all too often in our own society today. We are all involved to a greater or lesser extent in the process of dehumanisation. When we lie to each other, cheat on each other, twist and manipulate each other's emotions for personal advantage, what we are really doing is showing a contempt for our humanity and robbing ourselves of our dignity as those created in the image of God. And it has to be said that Christians can be as guilty as anyone in acting this way, and it is inexcusable in the sight of God.

God's contempt

In the second half of this chapter Job turns from the scandalous treatment he has received from men to the even more scandalous treatment he receives from God. More than once he has said some harsh and unwise things about God, but now he is so demoralised and miserable and in such bodily pain that he accuses God of being deliberately cruel towards him. 'And now my life ebbs away; days of suffering grip me. Night pierces my bones; my gnawing pains never rest. In his great power God becomes like clothing to me; he binds me like the neck of my garment. He throws me into the mud, and I am reduced to dust and ashes' (Job 30:16–19). Pain gnaws at his vitals continually, and it feels as if God has grabbed him by the collar, half-choking him. But he is not listening: 'I cry out to you, O God, but you do not answer; I stand up, but you merely look at me. You turn on me ruthlessly; with the might of your hand you attack me' (Job 30:20–21). He feels as helpless as a cork tossed about in stormy waters and is convinced that it will all end in death: 'You snatch me up and drive me before the wind; you toss me about in the storm. I know you will bring me down to death, to the place appointed for all the living' (Job 30:22–23).

Job's present misery

In view of God's attitude towards him, Job even questions whether his past life of spiritual integrity has been worth it, since God is not showing him the consideration he himself showed others in their distress. 'Surely no-one lays a hand on a broken man when he cries for help in his distress. Have I not wept for those in trouble? Has not my soul grieved for the poor? Yet when I hoped for good, evil came; when I looked for light, then came darkness' (Job 30:24–26). 'Is it worth it?' he is asking. 'I have done my best to serve God faithfully, and to treat others with respect and help them when I have been able, and all I get in return is scorn and contempt from both man and God. I get thrown in the mud like a piece of cast-off clothing and have to bear this dreadful pain day and night. The churning inside me never stops; days of suffering confront me. I go about blackened, but not by the sun; I stand up in the assembly and cry for help. I have become a brother of jackals, a companion of owls. My skin grows black and peels; my body burns with fever. My harp is tuned to mourning, and my flute to the sound of wailing' (Job 30:27–31).

It is all very sad, and terribly serious for Job to accuse God of treating him with contempt and being deliberately cruel towards him. But having said that, we hesitate to criticise him because we ourselves have had similar thoughts when suffering far less. On the other hand, we cannot make God the author of evil in our lives or believe that he deliberately abandons us and casts us off as his children. The whole thrust of the gospel is against such thinking. What is more, even when we are thinking or saying such harsh things about God, there is at the same time something inside us which persists in believing that it cannot be true. That was Job's experience. For in spite of all his accusations against God and the dreadful things he says, which would lead us to expect that he will ultimately reject God, he never does. He is still there at the end and says that he despises himself for the things he has said and repents in dust and ashes (Job 42:6).

So what is it that keeps us in the love of God even when we do not feel that we love him? What is it that keeps our faith intact, even when we feel it has broken down and failed? It can only be God himself. The Lord Jesus confirms this in that tremendously comforting statement of John's Gospel: 'And this is the will of him who sent me, that I shall lose none of all that he has given me, but raise them up at the last day' (John 6:39). This is the

From despair to hope

Chapter 24

doctrine of the eternal security of the believer. Our Lord is saying that when a man puts his faith in him and starts out on the Christian life, he need not fear that he will be unable to keep it up because of the down-drag of his sinful nature. Our Saviour will keep and protect him right through this earthly life, until he leaves this world and will be among all those raised up to be with Christ on the day of resurrection.

This means that we cannot lose our salvation when once we have it. When we belong to Christ, we belong to him for eternity. Our Lord confirms in another similar statement later on in John's Gospel, 'My sheep listen to my voice; I know them, and they follow me. I give them eternal life, and they shall never perish; no-one can snatch them out of my hand. My Father, who has given them to me, is greater than all; no-one can snatch them out of my Father's hand. I and the Father are one' (John 10:27–30). That is a great and wonderful promise. If Christ has saved us, then we shall never lose out on heaven and the joy of eternal life. We may be weak at times and even wander away from the path of truth and righteousness, but he will not lose his grip on us. Our perseverance rests not on our holding his hand, but on his hand holding ours. And however hard Satan and the ways of the world may try to pluck us out of his hand, they will fail. For he has given us his word that he will bring us through to the last day, when we shall be raised up at the resurrection into the glory of eternal life.

Chapter 25

Job's testimony of innocence

Read Job chapter 31

In chapter 29 Job had reminisced about the blessing and happiness he had enjoyed in past days. In chapter 30 he dwells upon the misery and suffering of his present situation, and now in this chapter he gives a personal testimony of his innocence to explain why his suffering is undeserved. On the face of it, it seems that he is being extremely self-righteous, because he talks of his own inner purity and goodness in God's sight. Indeed, some commentators come down on Job very heavily for that reason: 'He closes the mouths of his friends, he seems abundantly satisfied with himself; suppose God were to let it go at that, is the spectacle of the completely self-vindicated man a pleasant one? … At the close of it all Job is as far from God as at the beginning' (Samuel Ridout, Book of Job, pp. 165–6).

But this surely is to misunderstand Job's purpose in giving his testimony. He is not claiming righteousness in the sense of perfect goodness and sinlessness, but is simply vindicating his character in the light of the charges his friends have made against him. There is always a danger in giving public testimony to what God has done in one's life—it is open to misinterpretation. For that reason I must confess that I have not always been entirely happy with the practice of 'personal testimonies' in public, especially when given by a person young in the faith, for it can be dangerous and misleading. On the one hand, it can focus the attention of the listeners almost entirely upon the person testifying rather than upon God; on the other, it can give the impression of self-righteousness or a 'holier-than-thou' attitude. It seems that the apostle Paul was aware of this danger, for in 2 Corinthians he precedes his own testimony of what God had done in his life with the admission, 'In this self-confident boasting I am not talking as the Lord would, but as a fool' (2 Corinthians 11:17). However, we may understand this chapter not so much as Job's personal testimony to his friends of his innocence, but rather as simply his own pondering or meditation on the problem facing him.

Chapter 25

Job is saying in effect, 'Here is my life. I am prepared to take my stand on my personal moral and spiritual integrity before God, and I am confident he will judge me innocent of the charges that have been brought against me.' He then gives us an insight into seven areas of his life, from which we learn certain lessons.

Sexual immorality

In the area of sexual behaviour he says that he has never been guilty of deliberate lustful intention. 'I made a covenant with my eyes not to look lustfully at a girl. For what is man's lot from God above, his heritage from the Almighty on high? Is it not ruin for the wicked, disaster for those who do wrong? Does he not see my ways and count my every step?' (Job 31:1–4). Here he is anticipating in a remarkable way the words of our Lord centuries later: 'anyone who looks at a woman lustfully has already committed adultery with her in his heart. If your right eye causes you to sin, gouge it out and throw it away. It is better for you to lose one part of your body than for your whole body to be thrown into hell' (Matthew 5:28–29). A man may be led into sexual sin by allowing his eyes to linger on sexual images that stir the imagination and create in him a deliberate lustful intention. That is why advertisers make such a wide use of the sex angle to promote different commodities. Whether it is cars or a brand of soap makes little difference; beautiful girl models are brought into it somehow, because the visual impact of sexual images is extremely powerful.

CS Lewis says that the advertisers know that our sales resistance as consumers is weakened when the sex instincts are kept constantly aflame. He is absolutely right, and that is what makes pornographic magazines and sexually explicit films and television programmes so dangerous. They stimulate lustful intention. It is nonsense to say, as the so-called experts often do, that there is no correlation between exposure to this constant bombardment of sexual images and the sexual abuse and degrading of human sexuality that are so commonplace in today's society. Job is not condemning normal sexual desire, but he has a healthy fear of God's judgement upon the abuse of it, which keeps his steps from following the roving eye. 'Does he not see my ways and count my every step? If I have walked in falsehood or my foot has hurried after deceit ... if my steps have

Job's testimony of innocence

turned from the path, if my heart has been led by my eyes, or if my hands have been defiled, then may others eat what I have sown, and may my crops be uprooted' (Job 31:4–8). Still keeping to the area of sexual morality, Job affirms his faithfulness to the marriage relationship and declares that he has never allowed lustful intentions to entice him into an illicit relationship or to seduce another man's wife. 'If my heart has been enticed by a woman, or if I have lurked at my neighbour's door, then may my wife bring another man's grain, and may other men sleep with her. For that would have been shameful, a sin to be judged. It is a fire that burns to Destruction; it would have uprooted my harvest' (Job 31:9–12).

Here is a warning that the Christian community today needs to take to heart, since even among believers in evangelical churches adultery is no longer regarded as the heinous sin it once was. Yet here is Job saying that it is 'a sin to be judged. It is a fire that burns to Destruction.' And the writer to the Hebrews confirms this: 'Marriage should be honoured by all, and the marriage bed kept pure, for God will judge the adulterer and all the sexually immoral' (Hebrews 13:4). The truth is that adultery cheapens marriage, degrades human sexuality and brings untold misery and anguish into countless lives and families. And that is something God does not treat lightly.

Social justice

Job was a wealthy landowner with many servants to run his household and estate, and it would not have been so unusual in that day and age if he had treated them unkindly or even brutally. But he says he was not guilty of that. 'If I have denied justice to my menservants and maidservants when they had a grievance against me, what will I do when God confronts me? What will I answer when called to account? Did not he who made me in the womb make them? Did not the same one form us both within our mothers?' (Job 31:13–15). Whenever they had a complaint, even if it was against himself, his servants always received justice and fair play at his hands. And he gives two reasons for that: first, because of his sense of accountability to God at the judgement; second (and this is quite remarkable in that day and age), because of his belief in the equality of the human race in the sight of God. 'Did not he who made me in the womb make them?' He belonged to a different social stratum from his servants, but he did not allow any sense of

Chapter 25

superiority or class-consciousness to deny them their rightful dignity as God's creation. In this he was far ahead of his time. If we today would only see our fellow men as made in the image of God, there would be far less exploitation for personal advantage and profit, and human life would not be as cheap as it is.

Still with social justice and relationships in mind, Job says something about his attitude towards the poor and needy.

If I have denied the desires of the poor or let the eyes of the widow grow weary, if I have kept my bread to myself, not sharing it with the fatherless—but from my youth I reared him as would a father, and from my birth I guided the widow—if I have seen anyone perishing for lack of clothing, or a needy man without a garment, and his heart did not bless me for warming him with the fleece from my sheep, if I have raised my hand against the fatherless, knowing that I had influence in court, then let my arm fall from the shoulder, let it be broken off at the joint. For I dreaded destruction from God, and for fear of his splendour I could not do such things (Job 31:16–23).

He mentions three groups of unfortunate and dispossessed members of society: the poor, the widows and the orphans. Here were people who had no clout of any kind and were utterly dependent on what others could do for them. They are still with us today, certainly in the world as a whole: the hungry, the dispossessed and homeless, the orphans of the many war zones, the refugees endlessly trudging across frontiers seeking refuge. In spite of the advantages and progress of civilisation, for millions of people things have not changed a bit, and the need for the compassion Job showed is as great as ever it was. What motivated him in this direction was his reverence for God's holiness and splendour. 'For I dreaded destruction from God, and for fear of his splendour I could not do such things.' He means that if he had used his wealth and influence to deny the poor help and justice, he would come under the condemnation of God. Likewise we do a grave disservice to the gospel of Christ and deserve God's disapproval if we ignore the plight of the poor and needy in today's world.

Covetousness and greed

We have already said a good deal about Job's attitude towards material prosperity. Back in chapter 1 we are told, 'he owned seven thousand sheep, three thousand camels, five hundred yoke of oxen and five hundred donkeys, and had a large number of servants. He was the greatest man among all the people of the East' (Job 1:3). But now he is saying that he had never put his trust and confidence in his riches. 'If I have put my trust in gold or said to pure gold, "You are my security," if I have rejoiced over my great wealth, the fortune my hands had gained ...' (Job 31:24–25). Never at any time had the love for gold and the prestige and influence it could bring taken precedence over his love for God. He knew how to handle material prosperity and how to keep it in its proper place. Furthermore, he seems to be saying that he had not gained his wealth and position through his own efforts and power ('my hands') alone, thus implying that he owed it all to the goodness and mercy of God.

All this is not far from New Testament teaching about the place of riches in the Christian life. In the Sermon on the Mount our Lord warns us against covetousness and greed: 'Do not store [pile] up for yourselves treasures on earth' (Matthew 6:19). And he repeats it in his conclusion to the parable of the Rich Fool when he says, 'This is how it will be with anyone who stores up things for himself but is not rich towards God' (Luke 12:21). Paul in the same vein says, 'For the love of money is a root of all kinds of evil' (1 Timothy 6:10).

The gospel is not anti-materialist in the sense that it condemns the profit motive or material prosperity. But it does warn us again and again of the corrupting power of riches. 'For where your treasure is, there your heart will be also' (Matthew 6:21). It says in effect, 'Enjoy the good things of this life, but remember to keep them in their proper place. Show your gratitude to God by making his kingdom your treasure, and then money and the things money can buy will not hinder your Christian progress but will help you to bring glory to God.' John Wesley's dictum sums it up rather well: 'Get all you can, save all you can, give all you can.'

Idolatry

Job moves naturally from his attitude towards wealth to his attitude towards false gods and false worship. For money itself can become an idol for some people. In Colossians Paul makes mention of 'greed, which is

Chapter 25

idolatry' (Colossians 3:5). In the pagan environment of Job's day, people worshipped the heavenly bodies, but he himself never did, for it would have been a betrayal of his confidence in God. 'If I have regarded the sun in its radiance or the moon moving in splendour, so that my heart was secretly enticed and my hand offered them a kiss of homage, then these also would be sins to be judged, for I would have been unfaithful to God on high' (Job 31:26–28). We may think that we could never be enticed or seduced into the worship of the sun or moon or images of any kind, and therefore we are free from the peril of idolatry. But that is not so. For what is idolatry in essence? It is giving to anything in our lives the place and loyalty that rightly belong to God alone.

The principle of idolatry, therefore, can include almost anything. Paul mentions money, but it can be sex, sport, politics, career, home and family. I remember a man saying to me once, 'You know, I worship that boy of mine.' What he was saying was that he had an inordinate love for his 'boy' at the expense of his love for God. And that is the essence of idolatry; it is anything that becomes our ultimate concern and the end of all our striving, so that it absorbs our time and thought and energy to the exclusion of God. John ends his epistle with the words, 'Dear children, keep yourselves from idols' (1 John 5:21). It is a warning that all believers should thoroughly heed.

Vindictiveness

As a further evidence of his spiritual integrity, Job says that never at any time had he shown a spirit of vindictiveness or retaliation towards others, not even to those who were his enemies and may have done him harm. 'If I have rejoiced at my enemy's misfortune or gloated over the trouble that came to him—I have not allowed my mouth to sin by invoking a curse against his life' (Job 31:29–30). We are able to confirm the truth of this, since at the end of the book he is instructed by God to pray for the friends (enemies) who had treated him so shamefully and made such wild accusations against him, and he does so with very positive results. 'My servant Job will pray for you, and I will accept his prayer and not deal with you according to your folly' (Job 42:8).

All this comes very close to the teaching of the Lord Jesus about non-

Job's testimony of innocence

retaliation and loving one's enemies. 'You have heard that it was said, "Love your neighbour and hate your enemy." But I tell you, Love your enemies and pray for those who persecute you' (Matthew 5:43–44). This is a difficult thing to put into practice, but we need to work at it and ask God for grace to be able to do it, for the opposite is even worse. To cherish a spirit of revenge and bitterness towards others can be terribly destructive and do far more harm to the person who harbours it than to the one against whom it is directed. Vindictiveness and resentment can poison the whole moral system, distorting the personality, twisting and prejudicing our thinking and disrupting our fellowship with God. As long as we harbour a spirit of resentment in our heart we cannot be at peace with God. Paul urges us not to end the day in such a frame of mind. 'Do not let the sun go down while you are still angry, and do not give the devil a foothold' (Ephesians 4:26–27). The only wise thing to do with any feeling of resentment is to strangle it at birth.

Hospitality

Providing hospitality was regarded as an important duty among the nomadic people of the ancient world, and not to do so was looked upon as disgraceful. So important was it that if a stranger entered the home he was guaranteed the protection of the family. Lot's entertaining of the angels at Sodom is a good example of this: 'Don't do anything to these men, for they have come under the protection of my roof' (Genesis 19:8). Job says he was scrupulous in obeying the law of hospitality: 'If the men of my household have never said, "Who has not had his fill of Job's meat?"—but no stranger had to spend the night in the street, for my door was always open to the traveller' (Job 31:31–32). The New Testament is equally insistent in urging believers to practise hospitality. Peter says, 'Offer hospitality to one another without grumbling' (1 Peter 4:9). And when the Lord sent out the disciples to preach, he said that the refusal to give hospitality amounted to rejection of the gospel: 'If anyone will not welcome you or listen to your words, shake the dust off your feet when you leave that home or town. I tell you the truth, it will be more bearable for Sodom and Gomorrah on the day of judgment than for that town' (Matthew 10:14–15).

Are we hospitable? Do we see the provision of hospitality as a real

Chapter 25

ministry? Our homes can become strategic centres for the gospel: through providing hospitality for visiting preachers to the local church (3 John verses 5–8); as a means of witness, by inviting friends and neighbours to share a coffee and watch a Christian video; or as a base for study groups and other meetings. It is an interesting point that when Jesus talked on one occasion about the kingdom of God, he likened it to a great banquet at which God is the host and the guests are those who have accepted the invitation of the gospel (Luke 14:15–24).

Hypocrisy

Back in chapter 22 Eliphaz had strongly accused Job of hypocrisy, insisting that all his piety and godliness were a sham and a cover-up. But Job equally strongly denies the charge: 'if I have concealed my sin as men do, by hiding my guilt in my heart because I so feared the crowd and so dreaded the contempt of the clans that I kept silent and would not go outside …' (Job 31:33–34). He says that he had never used his religion as a cloak to cover his sins, or as a mask to hide behind for fear of incurring the wrath of the tribe if they discovered his transgressions. He had no need to do so, because his life was open before God and any transgressions he may have been guilty of had been repented of and forgiven.

One of the gravest charges our Lord made against the scribes and Pharisees was that of hypocrisy. In the Sermon on the Mount he says they were hypocritical in the matter of charitable giving, prayer and fasting (Matthew 6:1–18). In it all he is saying that they were pretending to be more spiritual or righteous than they really were. Likewise, the whole of Matthew 23 is a terrible denunciation of their hypocritical practices, and he warns the people, 'But do not do what they do, for they do not practise what they preach' (Matthew 23:3).

The man of the world, with all his faults, hates hypocrisy in all its forms. He hates it in public figures and politicians, when they make their ideological speeches but fail to put those ideals into practice. And he especially hates it in those who claim to be religious, when he sees them engaging in all the externals and outward forms of religion but not matching it with true godliness and a compassionate heart. As far as he is concerned it is all window dressing or acting a part, and nothing is more

Job's testimony of innocence

calculated to fill him with contempt for Christianity. In this respect the Church has a lot to answer for through the ages; and even today, in evangelical circles, this pseudo-spirituality is becoming increasingly evident and is a reproach to the gospel of Christ.

So Job's testimony of his innocence comes to a close, and we sense a note of confidence that God will vindicate him. 'Oh that I had someone to hear me! I sign now my defence—let the Almighty answer me; let my accuser put his indictment in writing. Surely I would wear it on my shoulder, I would put it on like a crown. I would give him an account of my every step; like a prince I would approach him' (Job 31:35–37). Symbolically, he is prepared to put his signature to all that he has said, so certain is he of his acquittal in God's sight. Furthermore, he calls upon God, again symbolically, to sign a writ of his innocence so that he might wear it proudly on his shoulder for all to see. On the other hand, the reference to writing could mean the accusations of his friends put in document form, which again he would wear 'like a crown', because he has already proved them to be empty, trumped-up charges and is confident God will see them as such. He even calls upon his land and the workers to bear witness to the falsity of the charges and to confirm his spiritual integrity: '"if my land cries out against me and all its furrows are wet with tears, if I have devoured its yield without payment or broken the spirit of its tenants, then let briers come up instead of wheat and weeds instead of barley". The words of Job are ended' (Job 31:38–40).

So he rests his case before God and is confident he will not be condemned. If there is one great truth to come out of this chapter it must surely be that our hearts should be full of thankfulness that, unlike Job, we do not have to prove our innocence before God in order to be free of condemnation. If we did, how many of us would make it? But that is the difference between law and grace. 'Therefore, there is now no condemnation for those who are in Christ Jesus, because through Christ Jesus the law of the Spirit of life set me free from the law of sin and death' (Romans 8:1–2).

Chapter 26

A young man speaks

Read Job chapter 32

This chapter opens by telling us that the verbal sparring between Job and the three friends has at last come to an end. 'So these three men stopped answering Job, because he was righteous in his own eyes.' Clearly they had given up on Job as a hopeless case, since they had failed to convince him with their arguments that he was suffering as a result of his sin. But we know that Job's refusal to budge from his position was not due to self-righteousness, but because in his heart he knew he was innocent before God. He loved God, believed God and was convinced that God knew him on the inside and would therefore vindicate him at the last.

Perhaps there is a lesson for us to learn here. Some Christians find it difficult to explain or defend their faith in words, and when in the company of clever non-Christians who engage in a form of mental bullying, seeking to undermine their faith with sophisticated and superior arguments, they tend to become confused and disheartened. But as long as they know the truth of God's salvation in their hearts, they have no need to be cowed by this display of intellectual arrogance or to budge from their position. In his own day, the apostle Paul dismisses the clever people who tried to destroy the simple faith of the Colossian believers with their 'fine-sounding arguments'. He describes their teaching as 'hollow and deceptive philosophy, which depends on human tradition and the basic principles of this world rather than on Christ' (Colossians 2:4,8). The fact is that one's own inner experience of the truth of God in Christ is far more compelling than all the specious and seductive arguments that are the product of the human mind. Job was confident in his heart that he was right with God, and that was all that mattered. But with the withdrawal of the three friends from the scene, another figure now enters the discussion in the person of Elihu.

A young man

'But Elihu son of Barakel the Buzite, of the family of Ram, became very angry with Job

A young man speaks

for justifying himself rather than God. He was also angry with the three friends, because they had found no way to refute Job, and yet had condemned him. Now Elihu had waited before speaking to Job because they were older than he. But when he saw that the three men had nothing more to say, his anger was aroused. So Elihu son of Barakel the Buzite said: 'I am young in years, and you are old; that is why I was fearful, not daring to tell you what I know. I thought, Age should speak; advanced years should teach wisdom' (Job 32:2–7).

Elihu, as we shall see, is a little bombastic and arrogant in his manner, but we can put that down to his lack of maturity. In spite of that, he seems to have been a likeable and courteous young man. His chief complaint at the outset is that he had not dared to intervene earlier, because convention dictated that the young should be seen rather than heard. 'Age should speak; advanced years should teach wisdom.' Sadly that is not always the case in real life. As we grow older, we should profit more and more from our experiences in life and as a result have a deeper understanding of its meaning and purpose, but it is not as straightforward as that. Men and women accumulate greater knowledge of many things as they grow older, but they are not necessarily wiser in their overall approach to life. We are all familiar with the saying, 'There is no fool like an old fool.' Elihu is right therefore when he says, 'It is not only the old who are wise, not only the aged who understand what is right' (Job 32:9).

This is especially true when we are dealing with spiritual matters and the things of God, such as Elihu is engaged in. He feels therefore that there is no reason why he should remain silent any longer. He too has a contribution to make, arising out of his own relationship with God. 'But it is the spirit in a man, the breath of the Almighty, that gives him understanding' (Job 32:8). The older men had relied entirely on human argument and insight to refute Job's position, but Elihu is saying that there is an insight and knowledge inspired by the Spirit of God working within a man. This is not so very different from what John says in his epistle to the believers of his day: 'But you have an anointing from the Holy One, and all of you know the truth' (1 John 2:20). There is a knowledge, an understanding that is independent of age and experience, and it comes from the indwelling Holy Spirit who gives insight into God's ways and purposes in the world. On this basis Elihu

Chapter 26

demands a hearing in spite of his youth. 'Therefore I say: Listen to me; I too will tell you what I know. I waited while you spoke, I listened to your reasoning; while you were searching for words, I gave you my full attention. But not one of you has proved Job wrong; none of you has answered his arguments. Do not say, "We have found wisdom; let God refute him, not man." But Job has not marshalled his words against me and I will not answer him with your arguments' (Job 32:10–14).

Elihu's insistence upon the right to speak about the things of God in spite of his immature years reminds us of Paul's words to Timothy: 'Command and teach these things. Don't let anyone look down on you because you are young, but set an example for the believers in speech, in life, in love, in faith and in purity' (1 Timothy 4:11–12). It seems that Timothy had a tendency as a young pastor to allow certain folk in the church to undermine his authority. But Paul is here reminding him that his authority is not related to his age, but to his call from God and the depth and reality of his faith in the Lord Jesus Christ. And that surely should be an encouragement to all Christians, whether young in years or young in their faith. God wants the contribution young people can make to the ongoing work of the Church. He wants their youth and vitality, their faith and enthusiasm.

An angry young man

It is clear from the opening verses that Elihu was also a very angry young man. 'But Elihu … became very angry with Job for justifying himself rather than God. He was also angry with the three friends, because they had found no way to refute Job … But when he saw that the three men had nothing more to say, his anger was aroused' (Job 32:2,3,5). His anger is more of a righteous indignation arising out of his brewing zeal and enthusiasm for the things of God. He feels that God's honour is at stake, because Job seems to have been justifying himself and because the three friends had not succeeded in defending God's character and justice. But we also get the feeling that if Elihu is not careful his angry feelings will get the better of him, and if that happens he will not be of much use as God's spokesman, neither will he be of much help to Job.

Now that is a very real danger with young people in the Christian life; their feelings and zeal and enthusiasm can run away with them and make them very angry with everyone and everything around them, especially in the life of the local church. They get angry with older Christians who appear to be rigid and inflexible, and slow to respond to the need for changes to make worship more exciting and stimulating. But they have to be reminded that older folk are sometimes sceptical of their enthusiasm because, being young, they have not yet proved that their zeal for the things of God is genuine and lasting and will not blow itself out in the short term. Let us go back for a moment to Paul's advice to Timothy: 'Don't let anyone look down on you because you are young.' That is good advice, but he then follows it up. He explains how Timothy is to get folk in the church to take him seriously in spite of his youth, and listen to what he has to say: 'set an example for the believers in speech, in life, in love, in faith and in purity.' Let young believers, then, prove to older folk in the church by their conduct and godliness of character that they can be taken seriously, and that their zeal is not of the 'frothy' variety that quickly dies down and blows itself out. Then, no doubt, they will be allowed to make their contribution to the church's work and witness.

An inner compulsion

Whatever his faults, one very attractive feature of Elihu's character is his overwhelming sense of the presence of God's Spirit within him. Speaking of the three friends he says: 'They are dismayed and have no more to say; words have failed them. Must I wait, now that they are silent ...? I too will have my say; I too will tell what I know. For I am full of words, and the spirit within me compels me; inside I am like bottled-up wine, like new wineskins ready to burst. I must speak and find relief; I must open my lips and reply' (Job 32:15–20). That is a graphic picture of a young man driven by a great inner compulsion to speak as the Spirit leads. It is not just a personal opinion he is expressing, but a word inspired by the Almighty. So great is this inner constraint to declare what God has given him that he feels like a new wineskin about to explode because of the wine fermenting within it.

This picture reminds us of two other men who were under a similar inner compulsion or constraint to declare the truth God had given them. At one point in his prophetic ministry Jeremiah, because of the hardness of people's hearts, was tempted to give up speaking on God's behalf. But it was

Chapter 26

no use; he simply could not keep quiet. 'But if I say, "I will not mention him or speak any more in his name, his word is in my heart like a fire, a fire shut up in my bones, I am weary of holding it in; indeed, I cannot' (Jeremiah 20:9). And Paul says: 'Yet when I preach the gospel, I cannot boast, for I am compelled to preach. Woe to me if I do not preach the gospel!' (1 Corinthians 9:16). There is a sense in which all true Christians should feel that same inner compulsion to speak to others of what God has done in their lives. We cannot remain silent when the opportunity arises to witness to the gospel; we should speak, not in any pressurised or vociferous manner, but with a feeling of urgency and seriousness that will make people listen.

For the preacher of the gospel this inner compulsion will be even stronger, and the members of the congregation will sense it. Effective exposition of the Word of God will not only inform the mind and stimulate the intellect, but it will also warm the heart and stir the emotions. There has to be some degree of passion in preaching, like Elihu's feeling of 'bottled-up wine'. This does not necessarily mean raising the voice or waving the arms, but there will be an earnestness that communicates itself to the hearers, making them realise that eternal issues are being dealt with, which for some are a matter of life or death. As Richard Baxter once said, 'I preached as never sure to preach again, as a dying man to dying men.'

Speaking to please God

Elihu makes it clear that what he has to say may not be the kind of thing that either Job or the friends may wish to hear, but that cannot be helped. His only concern is with the insight into God's truth that has been given to him, and therefore he speaks with a real sense of accountability and in the fear of God. 'I must speak and find relief; I must open my lips and reply. I will show partiality to no-one, nor will I flatter any man; for if I were skilled in flattery, my Maker would soon take me away' (Job 32:20–22). It is significant in this respect that when later, in the Epilogue (Job 42:7), God condemns the three friends for their attitude towards Job and because of some of the things they have said, he does not include Elihu in the condemnation.

When a preacher proclaims the Word of God, his first concern must not be to present the message in such a way that people will be flattered by it and find it acceptable. His concern is to proclaim God's truth, whatever people think of it. He will present the gospel message as winsomely as he can, but he will not distort it or tinker with it in order to make it more acceptable. He is not in the pulpit to please men but to please God. The apostle Paul warns the preachers of his day against this temptation: 'Therefore, since through God's mercy we have this ministry, we do not lose heart. Rather, we have renounced secret and shameful ways; we do not use deception, nor do we distort the word of God. On the contrary, by setting forth the truth plainly we commend ourselves to every man's conscience in the sight of God' (2 Corinthians 4:1–2). The preacher is there to point men and women to the Lord Jesus Christ for forgiveness and salvation, and he will do that with a real sense of accountability and in the fear of God.

Chapter 27

God's spokesman

Read Job chapter 33

Elihu still thinks of himself as God's spokesman as he now speaks directly to Job. Unlike the three friends, he addresses him by name. 'But now, Job, listen to my words; pay attention to everything I say. I am about to open my mouth; my words are on the tip of my tongue' (Job 33:1). He is clearly convinced in his own mind that what he has to say is worth saying, and that Job would do well to give him his undivided attention. He then touches on three things that should characterise anyone who speaks to others of the things of God, whether from a pulpit or in personal witness.

Speaking for God

First, it has to be evident that we are speaking from personal conviction. 'My words come from an upright heart', says Elihu (Job 33:3). He means simply that he believes fervently in what he is about to say. I disagree with those commentators who maintain that here we have a man who likes the sound of his own voice and who talks for the sake of talking. The reverse is true. Elihu has considered deeply what he is about to say and speaks out of the deep conviction of the Spirit of God within him. In the previous chapter he had referred to this inner constraint of the Spirit as 'bottled-up wine' (Job 32:19).

One of the pitiable and deplorable things in the Church today is the number of ministers who have long since lost their sense of conviction about the authority of the Word of God they are called upon to preach. To my mind there could be nothing more burdensome and intolerable than to have to enter a pulpit Sunday by Sunday to face a congregation with a message you no longer believe in with all your heart. How can any preacher hope to convince people of God's truth in that frame of mind? We must believe in our message and preach it with such fervency that people are left in no doubt that, for us at least, it is the greatest of all realities and is the very revelation of God in Christ. It is this sense of divine conviction on the part of the preacher, and the awesome responsibility that goes with it, that Peter has in mind when he says, 'If anyone speaks, he should do it as one speaking the very words of God' (1 Peter 4:11).

Second, people need to be aware that we have experienced in our own lives the truth we are speaking to them about: 'my lips sincerely speak what I know. The Spirit of God has made me; the breath of the Almighty gives me life' (Job 33:3–4). Elihu claims to speak from his own inner knowledge of God; the divine Spirit that first breathed into man also quickens and inspires him. It is this personal knowledge of God that gives confidence to our message and communicates itself to the hearers. Elihu's words, 'my lips sincerely speak what I know', remind us of the lines in Wesley's hymn,

> That which we have seen and heard
> With confidence we tell.

They also remind us of Paul's words, 'I know whom I have believed, and am convinced that he is able to guard what I have entrusted to him for that day' (2 Timothy 1:12). It is not enough that our message comes from an intellectual understanding, or a creed, or theology, or that our certainty in preaching rests on our own powers of persuasion. We must know God in his love and power and in the inward assurance of sins forgiven and the hope of eternal life.

Third, speaking with confidence and certainty of the things of Christ is right and proper; but we must never give those to whom we witness or preach the impression that we are different from them because God has saved us, and that we are experts in the matter of salvation. Elihu for all his brashness shows a very humble spirit when he says to Job, 'I am just like you before God; I too have been taken from clay. No fear of me should alarm you, nor should my hand be heavy upon you' (Job 33:6–7). He is saying in effect: 'Now, Job, I don't want you to think that I am speaking from a position of spiritual superiority. I am just as human as you are, made from the clay by God and having all the sins and failings you have, and I have no intention of coming down on you with a heavy hand and a holier-than-thou attitude.' And we can learn from that as preachers. We must, at all costs, avoid giving unbelievers in the congregation the impression that we are

Chapter 27

naturally religious and devout, and know nothing in our own lives of the moral defeats and struggles with sin and temptation that they encounter. In this respect authenticity is important, and people should know that we share the same humanity and feel the same down-drag of sinful nature as they do.

Of course, there has to be a balance in all this. In some evangelical circles today the emphasis has been to let this tendency for pastoral honesty develop into an emotional and spiritual dismantling in which the preacher bares all in a maudlin, sentimental kind of way. That is neither authentic nor God-honouring. It is enough to make it clear to those to whom we preach that we, like them, are sinful and unworthy, but that God in his grace and mercy has redeemed us through the precious blood of Christ, and that what he has done in us he can do in them.

Having made his preliminary remarks, Elihu now launches into his main address. He is chiefly concerned to vindicate God's character by reminding Job of certain things he had said and certain charges he had made which were deeply dishonouring to God.

The fact of sin

'But you have said in my hearing—I heard the very words—"I am pure and without sin; I am clean and free from guilt"' (Job 33:8–9). It is not true that Job had ever actually claimed to be sinless in God's sight, although he had refuted the notion that he was guilty of any sin so great that it had brought God's judgement upon him. Furthermore, he had always tried to live a faithful life and had asserted his moral integrity and uprightness. And God himself had acknowledged that fact: 'Have you considered my servant Job? There is no-one on earth like him; he is blameless and upright, a man who fears God and shuns evil' (Job 1:8).

Nevertheless Elihu is right to remind both Job and ourselves that however morally upright a man is, and however real his integrity, he can never claim to be sinless and free from guilt or think that God has no cause to find fault with him. Sin is an awful fact, and a man is deluding himself if he refuses to accept its reality in the human heart. As John says, 'If we claim to be without sin, we deceive ourselves and the truth is not in us' (1 John 1:8). Thousands are doing just that. They are deceiving themselves in denying the essential sinfulness of the human heart, and in the process, says John, they 'make him [God] out to be a liar' (1 John 1:10). The essence of their argument is that God's teaching in Genesis that the whole human race is tainted with the original sin of Adam is a gloomy view of human nature and one that they cannot accept. They say in effect: 'Don't believe God; don't believe his Word. He has got it all wrong; the human heart is not essentially corrupt. It may have its defects. People may do wrong things at times, and a few may be thoroughly bad. But, generally speaking, man is really good on the inside and, given time and the civilising influences of improved education and a better environment, he will eventually rid himself of the moral defects he now has and become the perfect being.'

That certainly is a delusion, since the corrupt nature of man stares us in the face wherever we look in our modern world. Indeed, it is in the Western democracies, where we have all these advantages in abundance, that the problems associated with a debased morality and with crime and violence are most acute. We have to acknowledge that sin is a malignancy that alienates man from his Maker and from his fellow men, and only God in Christ can deal with it.

If further proof were needed of the depravity of human nature, we have only to reflect on the events of Tuesday 11 September 2001, when the Western world was shaken by a crisis of phenomenal proportions. The World Trade Centre in New York was completely destroyed by terrorists with the loss of thousands of lives. The headlines at the time described it as 'a day that changed the world', and the American President referred to it as an 'attack on civilisation', and 'the first war of the twenty first century'. There is no doubt that it brought home to many of us, in the most dramatic way, that we are living at a time when our world seems to lurch from one crisis to another, and national upheavals, international strife, and natural disasters on a colossal scale force people to think more seriously about religious values and life's meaning.

It was not without significance that during that time of crisis, the churches both in America and here in our own country, were full of people seeking solace and comfort in prayer and worship. Special memorial services and national days of prayer were held which clearly indicated that at such time of crisis and heart-break, people instinctively felt that the only one they could turn to was the unchanging and eternal God. As the psalmist rightly says: 'God is our refuge and strength, an ever-present help in time of trouble. Therefore, we will not fear, though the earth give way and the mountains fall into the heart of the sea, through its waters roar and foam, and the mountains quake with their surging' (Psalm 46:1–3).

In the light of the tragedy that hit New York, there is something frighteningly modern about the Psalmist's description of the earth convulsing in a global catastrophy. It is heartening to know though that in the midst of such disaster, the Psalmist expresses his confidence in God as his refuge and help in trouble. It is to be hoped that the events of September 11 will help people to understand that it is not only during critical upheavals of life that we need to have God in our minds. He is always present and wants us to seek his help and power to meet even the ordinary circumstances of daily life.

God the enemy

Elihu continues to quote the dishonouring things Job had said about God. 'Yet God has found fault with me; he considers me his enemy. He fastens my feet in shackles; he keeps close watch on all my paths' (Job 33:10–11). Job had in fact said these things about God. Back in chapter 13 he complains: 'Why do you hide your face and consider me your enemy? … You fasten my feet in shackles; you keep close watch on all my paths by putting marks on the soles of my feet' (Job 13:24,27). He sees God as a celestial tyrant who has branded his feet like a slave to prevent him escaping. We must, however, make allowances for the fact that suffering and anguish such as Job was experiencing can so affect our thinking that even our understanding of God becomes distorted.

Elihu is right, nevertheless, to reprimand Job for speaking about God in this dishonouring way. 'But I tell you, in this you are not right, for God is greater than man' (Job 33:12). God is not a tyrant hounding man, watching him to detect his faults and failings, and preventing him from enjoying his life here below. If there is enmity between God and man, then it is all on man's side. It is man who sees God as his enemy and not the other way round. It is not God who needs to be reconciled to man, but man to God. Paul puts this very clearly in Romans 8:7–8 'the sinful mind is hostile to

God's spokesman

God. It does not submit to God's law, nor can it do so. Those controlled by the sinful nature cannot please God'. Sin has so distorted man's understanding of God that he does indeed see him as his enemy and therefore resists him at every turn, rejecting his overtures of love and the revelation of his saving mercy in the Lord Jesus Christ.

God's silence

A further complaint on Job's part which Elihu finds offensive is his assertion that God remains silent and does not answer his questions as to why he is suffering in the way he is. 'Why do you complain to him that he answers none of man's words?' (Job 33:13) It makes better sense to follow the NIV's alternative reading here: 'that he does not answer for any of his actions'. For that is exactly what Job was complaining about. He wanted God to come up with explanations as though he were accountable to man for what he does. But Elihu has already pointed out that 'God is greater than man' (Job 33:12). In short, we must allow God to be God, and not expect him to fit in with our reasoning as though he is under some obligation to explain his actions. We can understand Job's desire to obtain answers, but Elihu is right to remind us that as long as we adopt a confrontational attitude towards God, demanding answers from him, we shall know no peace. Paul makes the same point in Romans 9: 'But who are you, O man, to talk back to God? Shall what is formed say to him who formed it, "Why did you make me like this?" Does not the potter have the right to make out of the same lump of clay some pottery for noble purposes and some for common use?' (Romans 9:20–21). When the answers are not forthcoming we find our peace by resting in God's greatness.

God's communications

But God is not always silent. He is mindful of man's weakness and he does communicate with him in all manner of ways, says Elihu. 'For God does speak—now one way, now another—though man may not perceive it' (Job 33:14). The truth is that man is not always listening for God's voice or ready to accept that he has spoken. He then mentions two ways in which God speaks to men.

First, God communicates through dreams and visions. 'In a dream, in a

Chapter 27

vision of the night, when deep sleep falls on men as they slumber in their beds, he may speak in their ears and terrify them with warnings, to turn man from wrongdoing and keep him from pride, to preserve his soul from the pit, his life from perishing by the sword' (Job 33:15–18). Back in chapter 4, when dealing with the dream of Eliphaz, we said that we ought not to dismiss all talk of dream-communication and vision-revelation as fanciful and subjective, for that is how God made his purposes known to men. Both Old and New Testaments are full of such instances. God's intention in these communications was to warn men from going astray, as in the case of Abimelech (Genesis 20:3), or to keep man from pride in his own accomplishments, as in the case of Nebuchadnezzar (Daniel 4). And although it is open to God to use dreams and visions today to reveal his will, that is no longer the norm. We now have the complete revealed will of God in the Scriptures and in the person of Christ. 'In the past God spoke to our forefathers through the prophets at many times and in various ways, but in these last days he has spoken to us by his Son' (Hebrews 1:1–2). If we desire to know the mind of God and his purposes for the world and mankind, we must read and listen to his Word in the Scriptures, and not wait in the expectation of some special and dramatic revelation by way of dreams, or visions, or some other extraordinary spiritual phenomena.

Second, God communicates his purpose for a man through the use of suffering and illness. 'Or a man may be chastened on a bed of pain with constant distress in his bones, so that his very being finds food repulsive and his soul loathes the choicest meal. His flesh wastes away to nothing, and his bones, once hidden, now stick out. His soul draws near to the pit, and his life to the messengers of death' (Job 33:19–22). The picture is of a man in the last stages of a serious sickness, with death staring him in the face. Clearly Elihu must have had Job in mind, since the description fits his condition perfectly. But, unlike the three friends, he is not saying that Job's suffering is a punishment from God because of his sin, but rather that in his suffering God is wanting to teach him something.

And that is true. God does use sickness and the sufferings of this life to speak to us, or to chastise and discipline us. Under normal circumstances when we are strong and well and, as we think, in full control of the situation, we can be heedless of what God is saying to us. This can be the

God's spokesman

case with believers when their lives become so cluttered up with material pursuits that God's Word and the things of the soul become neglected and forgotten. Then sickness comes, and on that bed of pain God awakens them to the seriousness of their soul's condition and they become more receptive to what he has to say to them. In all this the divine purpose in the use of suffering is disciplinary and not punitive; it is preventative and seeks to keep us from making a shipwreck of our faith.

Restoration

But Elihu goes one step further and points out that God's ultimate purpose, even in allowing sickness, is the restoration of the backslider. 'Yet if there is an angel on his side as a mediator, one out of a thousand, to tell a man what is right for him, to be gracious to him and say, "Spare him from going down to the pit; I have found a ransom for him" then his flesh is renewed like a child's; it is restored as in the days of his youth. He prays to God and finds favour with him, he sees God's face and shouts for joy; he is restored by God to his righteous state' (Job 33:23–26). This is a wonderful and mysterious passage with strong Messianic overtones, for it speaks of an angelic mediator, the payment of a ransom and the restoration of man to his righteous state. These are all things relating to Christ and salvation.

However, not all commentators are agreed as to the identity of this angelic mediator or messenger. It could be a trusted and godly friend who is concerned to lead the sinner back from the error of his ways. In Job's case it could be Elihu himself. Likewise in our own case it is sometimes given to us to be the messenger of God to help in restoring a backsliding fellow believer and in that sense become for him 'one out of a thousand'. Isn't this what Paul had in mind when he says, 'Brothers, if someone is caught in a sin, you who are spiritual should restore him gently ... Carry each other's burdens, and in this way you will fulfil the law of Christ' (Galatians 6:1–2)? He is talking there about moral burdens or weaknesses associated with backsliding. But the mediating angel might indeed be some supernatural means or being that God uses to lead a sinner back into the way of righteousness. Again and again in the Old Testament we read of God's angel coming to men to reveal his will, to warn or to give guidance.

But the more we look at this passage, the more convincing it becomes

Chapter 27

that Elihu must have had in mind some dim understanding of the mediatorship of the Lord Jesus Christ and of his work in redemption. Elihu's words on the part of the mediator are a perfect expression of Christ's work in restoring the backslider and redeeming the sinner: 'one ... to be gracious to him and say, "Spare him from going down to the pit; I have found a ransom for him"' (Job 33:24). We can put that into the language of the New Testament: 'For there is one God and one mediator between God and men, the man Christ Jesus, who gave himself as a ransom for all men' (1 Timothy 2:5-6). In the verses that follow, Elihu in a remarkable way describes in wonderful language—the Christian significance of which he may not have fully understood—the sheer joy of the man or woman saved from sin and death. 'He prays to God and finds favour with him, he sees God's face and shouts for joy; he is restored by God to his righteous state. Then he comes to men and says, "I sinned, and perverted what was right, but I did not get what I deserved. He redeemed my soul from going down to the pit, and I shall live to enjoy the light." God does all these things to a man—twice, even three times—to turn back his soul from the pit, that the light of life may shine on him' (Job 33:26-30). Whether we have in mind the restored backslider, or the man who enters into the joy of salvation, those words have a perfect application to the saving work of the Lord Jesus Christ.

Elihu has more that he wants to say, but at this point he pauses to give Job an opportunity to reply. 'Pay attention, Job, and listen to me; be silent, and I will speak. If you have anything to say, answer me; speak up, for I want you to be cleared. But if not, then listen to me; be silent, and I will teach you wisdom' (Job 33:31-33). Clearly it is Elihu's desire to see Job restored to that position where he accepts God's dealings with him and is once more at peace—'for I want you to be cleared'. Job's silence, therefore, seems to indicate that he now accepts what is happening to him even though he may not understand it. And that is always the best place to come to in the end.

Chapter 28

The justice of God

Read Job chapter 34

Elihu, the eloquent young philosopher, is still in full flight. It is sometimes thought that the picture presented in this chapter is that of a courtroom scene, with Job as the defendant and Elihu the prosecutor. Elihu is appealing to the bystanders who had now gathered, and especially to the wise among them, to act as a jury in deciding who is right in the dispute between Job and himself. That may be true, although my own feeling is that Elihu is addressing in particular the three friends of Job and, in a more general sense, the wise and discriminating in every age. He is, after all, dealing with God's justice, and that is a principle that has universal application. 'Then Elihu said: "Hear my words, you wise men; listen to me, you men of learning. For the ear tests words as the tongue tastes food. Let us discern for ourselves what is right; let us learn together what is good"' (Job 34:1–4).

Discernment

Before entering on his speech concerning God's justice, Elihu appeals for his listeners to exercise a spirit of discernment in what they are about to hear. 'Let us discern for ourselves what is right; let us learn together what is good.' By 'right' and 'good' he has in mind moral and spiritual matters in relation to Job's attitude towards God. To make his point, he quotes a proverb used earlier by Job himself: 'Does not the ear test words as the tongue tastes food?' (Job 12:11). As the tongue discerns by taste whether what goes into the mouth is palatable or not, so the mind, in listening to the spoken word, should discern truth from error.

Writing to the Thessalonians Paul says: 'Do not put out the Spirit's fire; do not treat prophecies with contempt. Test everything. Hold on to the good. Avoid every kind of evil' (1 Thessalonians 5:19–22). They were not to accept every prophecy or message as if it were directed by the Holy Spirit, but they were to sift and test it in the light of what had already been revealed in the gospel. Similarly John urges his readers, 'do not believe every spirit,

Chapter 28

but test the spirits to see whether they are from God, because many false prophets have gone out into the world' (1 John 4:1).

All through the gospel age, this faculty of discernment in sifting what is true from what is false has been an indispensable requirement among God's people, and never more so than today. For false prophets and the spirit of anti-Christ are still with us, causing confusion and disillusionment in people's hearts and minds. This is one of Satan's main strategies, and we see it at work today in the scores of cults and pseudo-religions, such as Christian Science, the Mormons, the Moonies, Jehovah's Witnesses, the Spiritualist Church, Christadelphianism, the Church of Scientology, the peddlers of Astrology and the New Age movement. In addition, there are the false prophets of materialism and secularism, who deny the spiritual dimension of life; the humanists, who declare that man is the master of his own destiny; and the prophets of scientific rationalism, who tell us that man's salvation lies within the power of his own ability and intellect. But most dangerous of all, from the Christian standpoint, are the false prophets within the Church, the wolves in sheep's clothing of whom our Lord spoke. Like sheep they look outwardly harmless and perfectly acceptable, holding positions of trust and authority as pastors and teachers. You find them in pulpits, in bishops' chairs and in the theological faculties of our colleges and universities. They claim to speak for God, but in fact they undermine his truth, denying the basic doctrines of the Virgin Birth, the Divinity of Christ, the Atonement, the Resurrection, the Second Coming, Regeneration by the Holy Spirit and the veracity of the Bible.

In this welter of confusion, and with so many voices claiming to speak the truth, believers need to exercise discernment and to 'test the spirits to see whether they are from God', as John says. We do this by praying for the gift of discernment and by bringing everything to the bar of Holy Scripture and to the revelation given in the person of the Lord Jesus Christ.

Divine justice

Elihu now moves on to defend God's justice in the face of Job's accusations. 'Job says, "I am innocent, but God denies me justice. Although I am right, I am considered a liar; although I am guiltless, his arrow inflicts an incurable wound." What man is like Job, who drinks scorn like water? He keeps

The justice of God

company with evildoers; he associates with wicked men. For he says, "It profits a man nothing when he tries to please God"' (Job 34:5–9). He presents Job's words pretty fairly. Job had said, 'It is all the same; that is why I say, "He destroys both the blameless and the wicked"' (Job 9:22). And again, 'Though I cry, "I've been wronged!" I get no response; though I call for help, there is no justice' (Job 19:7). Commentators are not altogether agreed on what Elihu had in mind when he says that Job 'drinks scorn like water'. Some interpret these words to mean that Job is so hardened in his sin that he is impervious to the scorn and criticism heaped upon him. Others understand them to refer to Job speaking scornfully of God. I agree with this latter interpretation, as it fits better with Elihu's further charge that Job 'keeps company with evildoers; he associates with wicked men'. He does not mean that Job actually practises the evil of wicked men but that, by his scornful comments about God's unfairness and lack of justice, he places himself in the company of evildoers.

We can understand this, for sometimes as believers we too can be very scornful in the way we think and speak about God. When we are going through a difficult time like Job, and feel discouraged and depressed, we are not averse to speaking of God as being unfair, lacking justice, and treating us shabbily in allowing us to suffer in that way. But such opinions are those of the worldly irreligious person, and to entertain them is to 'walk in the counsel of the wicked' and to 'stand in the way of sinners' (Psalm 1:1). In vindication of the just character of God Elihu puts forward a number of arguments.

Exact retribution

God always treats a man as he deserves is his first argument. 'So listen to me, you men of understanding. Far be it from God to do evil, for the Almighty to do wrong. He repays a man for what he has done; he brings upon him what his conduct deserves' (Job 34:10–11). It is inconceivable to Elihu's mind that God should treat a man unfairly or do what is evil, since that would be a contradiction of the very nature of God. Man brings retribution upon himself for his actions, and that retribution is always in exact accordance with the deed. The Psalmist says to God, 'Surely you will reward each person according to what he has done' (Psalm 62:12). This

Chapter 28

same principle is expounded by our Lord in his picture of the narrow and broad roads, the one leading to life eternal and the other to destruction. Paul says the same thing in Galatians: 'Do not be deceived: God cannot be mocked. A man reaps what he sows. The one who sows to please his sinful nature, from that nature will reap destruction; the one who sows to please the Spirit, from the Spirit will reap eternal life' (Galatians 6:7–8).

This law of God's exact retribution will not allow men to make a mockery of his justice and his moral government of the world. A man reaps what he sows, either in blessing or punishment. Believers too are accountable to God in relation to this principle, and will receive whatever reward is due to them for the quality of their discipleship in this life. 'For we must all appear before the judgment seat of Christ, that each one may receive what is due to him for the things done while in the body, whether good or bad' (2 Corinthians 5:10). Elihu may have been a little over-zealous in stressing the doctrine of exact retribution, for he seems to be implying that Job deserved his suffering not because of sin, as the friends had insisted, but because of the contemptuous manner in which he had spoken of God's rule. For on more than one occasion (e.g. Job 9:23–24) Job had suggested that God is morally indifferent to whether men are good or bad. Elihu's point in refuting this position is this. Although the operation of the principle of exact retribution may not always be seen in this life, since the wicked sometimes seem to prosper and the innocent, like Job, reap trouble and hardship, nevertheless it is a principle in keeping with God's just character. And therefore everyone will ultimately receive the just reward for their deeds, either in this life or the next. Indeed, Job's own experience is itself a testimony to God's justice in this respect, since God rewarded him for his honesty and faithfulness with greater prosperity and blessing at the end of his life than anything he had known before.

God's supremacy

There would be no point in God being unjust and unfair in his treatment of the creation that he brought into being out of his love for mankind. That is Elihu's second argument. 'Who appointed him over the earth? Who put him in charge of the whole world? If it were his intention and he withdrew his spirit and breath, all mankind would perish together and man would

The justice of God

return to the dust' (Job 34:13–15). No one has delegated authority to God about how he should rule the world or deal with its people so that they can take him to task for not acting justly. He is supreme and in sole charge, and all life is sustained by him. If it were his intention, says Elihu, to treat man harshly and unjustly by withdrawing his Spirit, then mankind would be destroyed and God's purpose of love and fellowship for man would become meaningless.

At one point in the progress of the Reformation, when things were not going too well, Luther is reported as saying, 'If I were God and this world were as it is, I would knock it in pieces.' We can surely understand how he felt. The world of mankind, with its violence and stupidity and hatred, can be so ugly and unjust at times that we feel the only thing it deserves is to be knocked in pieces. How thankful we should be, therefore, that God, who has the power to knock the world in pieces, does not do that! Instead, he has revealed his great love for mankind in the gospel of Christ and tempered his justice with mercy in the offer of forgiveness. To quote Vernon Higham's hymn:

> Great is the gospel of our glorious God,
> Where mercy met the anger of God's rod;
> A penalty was paid and pardon bought,
> And sinners lost at last to Him were brought.

God's impartiality

Elihu moves on to his third argument in refutation of Job's complaint that God is not just. 'If you have understanding, hear this; listen to what I say. Can he who hates justice govern? Will you condemn the just and mighty One? Is he not the One who says to kings, "You are worthless" and to nobles, "You are wicked," who shows no partiality to princes and does not favour the rich over the poor, for they are all the work of his hands? They die in an instant, in the middle of the night; the people are shaken and they pass away; the mighty are removed without human hand' (Job 34:16–20).

In meting out justice to men God is totally impartial. He is not swayed in his judgement by a man's rank, wealth or status. He has no favourites and

Chapter 28

treats all alike because 'all are the work of his hands'. He gave man the gift of life and, when it pleases him, he can take that life away; and no amount of wealth or position in society can persuade him otherwise. Job himself is a good example of God's impartiality, since his wealth and social standing did not prevent God from inflicting suffering on him. All this comes very close to the gospel, as illustrated by our Lord's parable of the Rich Fool (Luke 12) and especially as given by James in his epistle: 'My brothers, as believers in our glorious Lord Jesus Christ, don't show favouritism' (James 2:1). His reason for urging this is that God has no favourites but is totally impartial in giving the gift of salvation. 'Listen, my dear brothers: Has not God chosen those who are poor in the eyes of the world to be rich in faith and to inherit the kingdom he promised to those who love him?' (James 2:5). Paul makes the same point: 'Brothers, think of what you were when you were called. Not many of you were wise by human standards; not many were influential; not many were of noble birth' (1 Corinthians 1:26).

The personal implications of God's impartial justice in the matter of salvation are both profound and easy to see. Do I deserve God's forgiveness and the gift of eternal life? Am I better than others? Am I worth saving more than others? I am forced to admit, as I look at my own heart, that if salvation depended upon God's partiality or favouritism, then I am doomed, for there is nothing in my life I can conceive of that merits preferential treatment. It is all of God's grace and mercy, whoever we are.

God's omniscience

One of the greatest attributes of God is his omniscience: he sees and knows everything. This is the basis for Elihu's fourth argument in support of God's justice: 'His eyes are on the ways of men; he sees their every step. There is no dark place, no deep shadow, where evildoers can hide' (Job 34:21–22). If he knows everything about us and sees everything we do, so that the wicked can find no hiding place for their misdeeds, then surely God's justice can be relied upon, because his judgements are not based on ignorance of the facts. He does not have to probe or examine a man or hold a public enquiry to find out what he is up to. 'God has no need to examine men further, that they should come before him for judgment. Without enquiry he shatters the mighty and sets up others in their place' (Job

34:23–24). The wicked think they can get away with their wickedness; but God in his justice takes note of every deed and sees every action, and one day he will punish them for their wickedness. 'Because he takes note of their deeds, he overthrows them in the night and they are crushed. He punishes them for their wickedness where everyone can see them, because they turned from following him and had no regard for any of his ways. They caused the cry of the poor to come before him, so that he heard the cry of the needy' (Job 34:25–28).

Finally, Elihu meets Job's earlier complaint that God remains silent (Job 24:12) when the cries of the dying and dispossessed come up before him, instead of exercising his justice by punishing those responsible. 'But if he remains silent, who can condemn him? If he hides his face, who can see him? Yet he is over man and nation alike, to keep a godless man from ruling, from laying snares for the people' (Job 34:29–30). Elihu is saying there that we cannot condemn God for his silence and inaction, for we can only see in part and not the whole. But God in his omniscience sees everything in the lives of men and nations and will mete out justice when the time is right.

It came as a wonderful discovery to the Psalmist that God knew all about him down to the tiniest detail in his life. 'O Lord, you have searched me and you know me. You know when I sit and when I rise; you perceive my thoughts from afar. You discern my going out and my lying down; you are familiar with all my ways' (Psalm 139:1–3). It amazed him that within this vast universe his personal life came under the scrutiny of the eternal God, who knew his past, present and future. For the wicked person this is frightening, but for the believer it holds no fear, because the evil things God sees in us have already been forgiven and are covered by the righteousness of Christ. 'Therefore, there is now no condemnation for those who are in Christ Jesus, because through Christ Jesus the law of the Spirit of life set me free from the law of sin and death' (Romans 8:1–2). Furthermore, although we still give way to temptation and fall into sin, God also knows that we hate ourselves for doing so. He also knows our inner desires after truth and holiness, and that too brings comfort to our hearts.

A word of counsel

Having set out his arguments in defence of God's justice, Elihu now

Chapter 28

counsels Job on what he should do and urges him to repent of the offensive statements he has made concerning God's character. 'Suppose a man says to God, "I am guilty but will offend no more. Teach me what I cannot see; if I have done wrong, I will not do so again." Should God then reward you on your terms, when you refuse to repent? You must decide, not I; so tell me what you know' (Job 34:31–33). Job is being urged to make clear his position in relation to God's rule. If he acknowledges his guilt in challenging God's rule as he has done, then he should repent and resolve not to make the same mistake again. But if he refuses to repent, he is saying that God has got it wrong and that he should rule according to Job's terms and Job's way of thinking.

This is wise counsel, however you look at it. So often we ourselves need to pray, 'Teach me what I cannot see.' In our own life's experience we fail at times to understand or 'see' exactly what God is about, or what he is doing in us, and we need his help. What it comes down to in the end is this. Do we want God to run this world and deal with its people according to his terms and his justice, or according to our terms and our idea of justice? Elihu is convinced that Job has adopted the latter position, and he turns to the friends for confirmation of this: 'Men of understanding declare, wise men who hear me say to me, "Job speaks without knowledge; his words lack insight." Oh, that Job might be tested to the utmost for answering like a wicked man! To his sin he adds rebellion; scornfully he claps his hands among us and multiplies his words against God' (Job 34:34–37).

On the face of it Elihu's request that 'Job might be tested to the utmost for answering like a wicked man' sounds excessively cruel—as if he were wanting Job's suffering to be extended because of his wickedness. But in fact he is simply wanting Job's trial to be the means of bringing him to humble repentance and the strengthening of his understanding of God's ways. It is not unlike the statement of Peter concerning spiritual trial. 'These have come so that your faith—of greater worth than gold, which perishes even though refined by fire—may be proved genuine and may result in praise, glory and honour' (1 Peter 1:7). In Job's case this, in fact, is what actually happened. There came a point when he did accept Elihu's charge that 'his words lack insight' and he humbly repented of it. In the last chapter of the book he says to God, 'Surely I spoke of things I did not understand, things too wonderful for me to know ... Therefore I despise myself and repent in dust and ashes' (Job 42:3,6).

We must reiterate something we said earlier, namely, that Elihu's indictment of Job is not to be confused with that of the friends. They had condemned Job because they were convinced that he was guilty of some grave sin before God and was being punished because of that. Their counsel was that Job should confess and repent of his sin and receive once again God's blessing on his life. But that would have meant on Job's part a measure of deception, since he would have been repenting of something of which he was not guilty in order to gain forgiveness. Had he done so, he would have been guilty of the very thing Satan, at the outset, had accused him of before God—that his service and devotion were based entirely on self-interest: 'Does Job fear God for nothing?' (Job 1:9). Elihu on the other hand is concerned not with discovering the cause of Job's suffering, whether because of sin or anything else, but to defend the just character of God and his righteous government of the world. He condemns Job because of his rebellious refusal to accept that it is inconceivable that God should pervert justice in the slightest degree, and that is why he advises him to repent.

The question that faces all of us is this. Are we prepared to accept that God, with his superior wisdom and power, must be allowed to govern this world according to his own rule of justice? Or do we ignore his rule and run our lives according to our own rules; and if so, are we prepared to accept the consequences? Each of us must decide that for himself. Looking at the mess our world is in we have to acknowledge that a great many people are saying, in the words of the song, 'I'll do it my way', and are ignoring God.

Chapter 29

Does it pay to serve God?

Read Job chapter 35

In this chapter Elihu still has in mind Job's complaint concerning God's justice, and in particular his assertion that there is no advantage in living a godly life. 'Then Elihu said: "Do you think this is just? You say, 'I shall be cleared by God.' Yet you ask him, 'What profit is it to me, and what do I gain by not sinning?'"' (Job 35:1–3).

The profit of godliness

Job was convinced that God was being unjust in his treatment of him, but now Elihu turns the whole question of justice back on Job. He asks him if he was being just and consistent in saying, on the one hand, 'I shall be cleared [vindicated] by God' and, on the other hand, in complaining that there is no profit or value in refraining from sin and living a godly life. For Job had in fact said these things about God. Earlier he had charged God with being morally indifferent to what happens in the world. 'The groans of the dying rise from the city, and the souls of the wounded cry out for help. But God charges no-one with wrongdoing' (Job 24:12). He is thus implying that there is nothing to be gained by living a righteous life.

But is that true? And have we ourselves ever felt like that in our low moments? Have we questioned the value of serving God in Christ, when we have looked around and seen other people who are not believers living seemingly full and satisfying lives? Have we been tempted to think within ourselves, 'Where is the advantage in trying to live for God in a world like ours? What is the point in trying to be honest and truthful and putting Christ at the centre of my life? Where has it got me in the end, and does it make any difference whether I believe in God or not?' Speaking on behalf of himself and the other disciples, Peter put the same question directly to Christ himself: 'Peter answered him, "We have left everything to follow you! What then will there be for us?"' (Matthew 19:27). Was he simply being mercenary-minded?

In his reply to Peter our Lord makes it perfectly clear that there are

Does it pay to serve God?

wonderful compensations or rewards in Christian discipleship. '"I tell you the truth," Jesus replied, "no-one who has left home or brothers or sisters or mother or father or children or fields for me and the gospel will fail to receive a hundred times as much in this present age (homes, brothers, sisters, mothers, children and fields—and with them persecutions) and in the age to come eternal life"' (Mark 10:29–30). In short, Jesus is saying that it does indeed pay to serve God, both in this life and in the life to come. Christian discipleship is a mixture of triumph and persecution, of blessing and suffering; but through it all the Christian can never make God his debtor. If he loses one set of friends in the world by committing his life to Christ, he can rest assured that he will make a hundred more by being part of the family of God. And there are the spiritual rewards of being at peace with God in one's heart, enjoying the forgiveness of sins and the leading and guiding of the Holy Spirit in daily life. But, over and above all these things, there is the greatest of all rewards in the certainty that heaven is our home and that one day we shall be in the presence of God where there are pleasures for evermore.

> There is a land of pure delight,
> Where saints immortal reign;
> Infinite day excludes the night,
> And pleasures banish pain.

God and ourselves

Having remonstrated with Job because of the ridiculousness of his position in questioning the value of living to please God, Elihu now directs him to consider God's greatness as the creator and sustainer of all things. 'Look up at the heavens and see; gaze at the clouds so high above you. If you sin, how does that affect him? If your sins are many, what does that do to him? If you are righteous, what do you give to him, or what does he receive from your hand?' (Job 35:5–7). He is wanting to get over to Job the idea that God is so different from ourselves, and so far above us in his greatness, that nothing we do or say can affect him in any way. Eliphaz had used a similar argument back in chapter 24.

Chapter 29

But in repeating it Elihu seems to be saying something like this. 'Now, Job, look up to the heavens and start getting your thinking straight where this mighty Creator God of ours is concerned. You have been talking about whether or not it is profitable to serve him. But the really important question is not whether you get any benefit or profit out of serving God, but does God get any benefit or profit out of your serving him? Is there anything you can give to God that will enlarge his being or extend his greatness in any way? And do you think that your wretchedness and sin can affect his character or influence his actions? You must get it into your head that "Your wickedness affects only a man like yourself, and your righteousness only the sons of men" (Job 35:8), and has no effect upon God.'

Elihu is right in what he says. We must never get into the habit of thinking that our holiness of life or moral standing can so influence God that it gives us some kind of bargaining position. In other words, we say in effect: 'Now, Lord, here I am living my Christian life, endeavouring to avoid what is sinful, and seeking to do what is right and good, as the gospel states. And since I am doing all this for your benefit, you in turn must do something for me. I want some profit from following Christ. I don't want any problems or difficulties, but I want my life to run smoothly and pleasantly. Surely you can do that for me?' Of course we do not actually talk to God like that, but we do have a tendency to think that if we live our lives in faithful service, then God owes us something or is under some obligation to us. But the Lord Jesus taught the very reverse of that. In his parable about the servant who had worked hard all day and then had to provide a meal for his master before dragging his tired body to bed, he concludes by saying this: 'So you also, when you have done everything you were told to do, should say, "We are unworthy [unprofitable] servants; we have only done our duty"' (Luke 17:10).

The point Jesus is making is that even when we have done our very best, we can never fulfil our obligation to God. I am to worship and adore God because of what he is in himself, the mighty Creator God, and not because of anything I get from him because my service is profitable. Our worship and service are the response of our own worthlessness and nothingness to his loving mercy and saving grace shown to us in the Lord Jesus Christ.

Does it pay to serve God?

> Were the whole realm of nature mine,
> That were an offering far too small;
> Love so amazing, so divine,
> Demands my soul, my life, my all.

Perplexities in prayer

The final section in this chapter (verses 9–16) is a difficult one to understand, but it seems that Elihu's main concern is with the problem of unanswered prayer. 'Men cry out under a load of oppression; they plead for relief from the arm of the powerful. But no-one says, "Where is God my Maker, who gives songs in the night, who teaches more to us than to the beasts of the earth and makes us wiser than the birds of the air?"' (Job 35:9–11). His first point is this. When men cry out to God in their suffering, they do so not because they really trust God, believing that he can give them grace and strength in the dark night of trouble, and that he cares for them more than he does the animal creation, but because they resent what is happening to them and desire only to be delivered from it. Elihu says this because Job, more than once, had complained that God does not respond to the cries of the poor and oppressed (Job 24:12) and in his own prayers had complained to God 'in the bitterness of my soul' (Job 10:1). But prayers asked in a spirit of resentfulness and bitterness rather than in a spirit of humble faith can never hope to be answered. This is the lesson James has in mind when he says, 'When you ask, you do not receive, because you ask with wrong motives, that you may spend what you get on your pleasures' (James 4:3). Paul and Silas, on the other hand, did the very thing Elihu suggests: they sang praises to God in their dark night of trouble, and God answered them. 'About midnight Paul and Silas were praying and singing hymns to God, and the other prisoners were listening to them. Suddenly there was such a violent earthquake that the foundations of the prison were shaken. At once all the prison doors flew open, and everybody's chains came loose' (Acts 16:25). Prayers must be made in a right spirit if they are to be answered.

Elihu takes his argument a step further by saying that God will not listen to prayer when it is asked in a spirit of pride and arrogance. 'He does not

Chapter 29

answer when men cry out because of the arrogance of the wicked. Indeed, God does not listen to their empty plea; the Almighty pays no attention to it' (Job 35:12–13). He is saying that men adopt an arrogant attitude in prayer, thinking they can call upon God to serve their personal convenience, and that he is always obliged to help them in their troubles. And there is no doubt that people do this all the time. They hardly ever give a thought to God, but when suddenly they hit an emergency they call upon him and, in their arrogance, expect him to get them out of the mess they are in. But Elihu is saying that we cannot treat God in that shabby, arrogant manner; God is not like the Emergency Services to be called upon only when we are in trouble. He then turns to Job and says that he has been guilty of treating God in that arrogant way. 'How much less, then, will he listen when you say that you do not see him, that your case is before him and you must wait for him, and further, that his anger never punishes and he does not take the least notice of wickedness' (Job 35:14–15).

It is true that Job had, in fact, adopted at times a high-handed attitude towards God. He had complained that he lacked justice, did not care for the poor, was indifferent to whether men were righteous or wicked, and that he kept him waiting for an answer to his own particular problem of suffering. We must, of course, make allowances for the fact that Job in his deep depression and distress was giving vent to his feelings, and that in more normal circumstances he would never talk about God in that way. Nevertheless, as long as he was in that wrong spirit he could never expect his prayers to be answered, and that is why Elihu concludes: 'So Job opens his mouth with empty talk; without knowledge he multiplies words' (Job 35:16).

In the light of all this we are bound to say, however, that the subject of prayer raises for many of us all kinds of perplexing questions. We do not understand the mechanics of prayer, how it works; but as believers we find we cannot do without it any more than our body can do without oxygen. It is an absolute necessity. Furthermore, we do not have to understand all the perplexities associated with prayer before we engage in it. And this has been the experience of God's people even when they have been at their most unspiritual: for example, Samson between the pillars of Dagon's temple (Judges 16:28) or king Saul offering the sacrifice in disobedience (1 Samuel

Does it pay to serve God?

13:9). For it is not only believers who feel the need of prayer. In the Second World War the saying was, 'There are no atheists in foxholes.' When a man in combat was hiding in a hole in the ground, with shells bursting all around him, he would suddenly find himself praying, even if he had never given much thought to God before.

We also engage in prayer because the Bible commands it. In his Sermon on the Mount the Lord Jesus says, 'And when you pray, do not be like the hypocrites' (Matthew 6:5). He clearly takes it for granted that his followers make prayer a regular practice in their daily lives. In Luke 18 the reason he gives for his parable of the Persistent Widow is 'that they should always pray and not give up'. Paul in giving instructions to the Thessalonian church says, 'pray continually', reminding us to make prayer a priority and to appreciate the privilege of being able to engage in it at any time of day or night, and in any place. For we do not always need to verbalise our prayers, but we can be thinking prayerfully when engaged in other things.

One thing that perplexes people about prayer is why we need to do it when God knows in advance what our needs are. After all, we cannot inform God of anything he does not know already. The answer might be that whilst God meets the majority of our needs without our having to ask for them, such as food, shelter and so on, there are other things he has decided in his wisdom that we must ask for in prayer. Perhaps the reason for this is that it serves to emphasise the important place prayer should have in the discipline of our daily lives.

Another important feature in prayer is that it can actually help to strengthen God's hand in the warfare against the powers of darkness. With this in mind Paul says, 'The weapons we fight with are not the weapons of the world. On the contrary, they have divine power to demolish strongholds' (2 Corinthians 10:4). The strongholds are those of Satan, and the prayers of believers are mighty weapons in God's arsenal for their destruction. William Cowper puts it like this:

> And Satan trembles when he sees
> The weakest saint upon his knees.

But undoubtedly, for the Christian, the greatest perplexity associated with

Chapter 29

prayer is that raised by Elihu—the problem of 'unanswered' prayer. In addition to the explanations given by Elihu, we might also say that the unanswered prayer is God in his wisdom saying no to our request, and that that in itself is the answer. Sometimes the prayer seems to be unanswered, whereas in fact God for his own reasons may be delaying the answer. We have a good example of this in the story of Zechariah and Elizabeth in Luke 1. For years they had been praying for a child and nothing happened. But when they were both old, and past the age of child bearing (Luke 1:7), God says, 'your prayer has been heard. Your wife Elizabeth will bear you a son' (Luke 1:13). Commenting on this, Matthew Henry says, 'Prayers of faith are filed in heaven and are not forgotten, though the thing prayed for is not presently given.' The thing to remember is that unless we receive a definite negative from God, we should keep on praying and wait patiently for God's own time.

Chapter 30

God, man and nature

Read Job chapters 36 and 37

These two chapters ought never to have been separated in our Bibles as, together, they form Elihu's final speech to Job. Furthermore, it will be noticed that they have been separated in entirely the wrong place—in the middle of Elihu's magnificent description of God's mighty power at work in nature in the form of a thunderstorm. Speaking of a similarly unskilful separation of chapters in another part of the Bible, Spurgeon says that the person responsible must have used a 'meat-axe'!

Faith concealed

Elihu is still concerned to vindicate the character of God and the justice of his dealings with man and nature. He begins by requesting Job to be patient with him a little longer because there are still further spiritual insights he wants to bring to his attention. 'Elihu continued: "Bear with me a little longer and I will show you that there is more to be said on God's behalf"' (Job 36:1–2). He has already said plenty about God's ways, but he is not finished yet by a long shot! Is he then just a windbag who likes the sound of his own voice? There are those writers who say he is exactly that; they describe him as pretentious, overconfident and arrogant, and say that it would have been better had he not spoken at all. But the truth is surely that there is always 'more to be said on God's behalf', and there are not nearly enough Christians who are prepared to say it!

Why is it that so many believers today are somehow reluctant to speak of their faith in God and their acceptance of Christ as Lord and Saviour? Is it because we fear the ridicule of others or that it will make us unpopular in some way? But even if that were to happen, it is a small price to pay in return for what God has done in bringing us out of the darkness of sin and ignorance into the light of his truth and salvation. I am reminded here of the incident of the woman in the crowd who touched the edge of the Lord's cloak and was healed. She hoped to conceal her action and remain unobserved. 'But Jesus said, "Someone touched me; I know that power has

From despair to hope 187

Chapter 30

gone out from me." Then the woman, seeing that she could not go unnoticed, came trembling and fell at his feet ... Then he said to her, "Daughter, your faith has healed you. Go in peace"' (Luke 8:46–48). She had received his power of healing, but had concealed it until Jesus insisted that she glorify God openly. As Hendriksen puts it, 'Faith concealed became faith revealed' (Gospel of Luke, p. 465). That is one reason why we should not be secretive about our Christian discipleship, because it grieves God's Spirit and denies him the glory that is rightfully his. Furthermore, ours is a very vocal age, when people representing a variety of opinions are making their voices heard. The homosexual movement, the hunt lobby, the anti-hunt lobby, the Friends of the Earth, the so-called 'progressives' in morals and education, the exponents of the New Age philosophy, the animal rights activists—all these have more to say on their own behalf, and they are saying it loudly and clearly. Why shouldn't the believer likewise make his voice heard, especially when what he has to say is of such great significance, because it is on God's behalf?

Knowledge of God

But how do we get our knowledge of God? Elihu says, 'I get my knowledge from afar; I will ascribe justice to my Maker. Be assured that my words are not false; one perfect in knowledge is with you' (Job 36:3–4). Some interpret the statement 'I get my knowledge from afar' as referring to the breadth or range of spiritual truth Elihu had dealt with. And it could well mean that, since he had touched on many truths apart from God's justice. Likewise we ourselves must not get hung up on one particular aspect of eternal truth. Some preachers are forever dealing with the same thing: the sovereignty of God or the Second Coming or the person and work of the Holy Spirit or Election, and so on. But we need a breadth to our preaching, ranging over a wide area of biblical truth and involving different types of preaching: expository, narrative, parable, life situation, doctrinal and topical. However, it is much more probable that by the expression 'I get my knowledge from afar' Elihu really means that his spiritual understanding comes from God himself, in the way the Psalmist speaking of God says, 'he knows from afar' (Psalm 138:6). And when he says, 'one perfect in knowledge is with you', he is not being arrogant and conceited. He simply means that the truth of God he is speaking about is perfect; he is not going to talk about things that are the product of his own shallow thinking and opinions.

All too often that is the kind of thing we hear from our pulpits today: the opinions and thoughts of men rather than the truth of God enshrined in his Word. But people are not saved from sin and damnation by our ideas and theological speculations, however erudite or eloquently presented. And they most certainly will not be won to Christ through the kind of sermon that is little more than a string of anecdotes and amusing stories held together with a few moralistic platitudes. We have the whole Bible to preach from, and it is only as we expound its message faithfully with the help of the Holy Spirit that people will be brought into an understanding of the knowledge of God and his salvation. As Paul says, 'My message and my preaching were not with wise and persuasive words, but with a demonstration of the Spirit's power, so that your faith might not rest on men's wisdom, but on God's power' (1 Corinthians 2:4–5).

The God of might and compassion

Elihu has already informed Job that 'there is more to be said on God's behalf'. First to be looked at among these additional truths is the might and compassion of God. 'God is mighty, but does not despise men; he is mighty, and firm in his purpose. He does not keep the wicked alive but gives the afflicted their rights. He does not take his eyes off the righteous; he enthrones them with kings and exalts them for ever' (Job 36:5–7). The fact that God is mighty in power and strength, so that no one can successfully challenge or oppose his rule and defeat his purpose, does not mean that he despises men or treats them as of no account. All men have worth and significance in his sight because they are part of his creation and are made in his own image. Job especially needed to be reminded of this because earlier, in the depths of his misery, he had asked God, 'Does it please you … to spurn the work of your hands?' (Job 10:3). And we need to be reminded of it, because it gives meaning and significance to our own lives to know that God, the mighty Creator, does not despise or spurn our individual place in the vast scheme of things. This is particularly true of believers, who have a special place in the love and compassion of God. 'Are not two

Chapter 30

sparrows sold for a penny? Yet not one of them will fall to the ground apart from the will of your Father. And even the very hairs of your head are all numbered. So don't be afraid; you are worth more than many sparrows' (Matthew 10:29–31).

But the fact that God does not despise any of his creatures does not mean either that he fails to make any distinction between the righteous and the wicked. In his perfect justice 'He does not keep the wicked alive' (Job 36:6)—that is, he does not put up with sin and rebellion indefinitely, but sooner or later he will bring his judgement upon them, either in this life or the next. Let us not think for one moment that those guilty of wrongdoing ever get away with it. But God watches over his own in their afflictions and 'does not take his eyes off the righteous; he enthrones them with kings and exalts them for ever' (Job 36:7). This is a figurative way of saying that in his compassion and mercy God will never forsake his people. However despised and lowly they may be in the eyes of the world, they are exalted in his eyes and enjoy the status of belonging to the royal family of God. We can put all this in New Testament language: 'To him who loves us and has freed us from our sins by his blood, and has made us to be a kingdom of priests to serve his God and Father—to him be glory and power for ever and ever! Amen' (Revelation 1:5–6).

God's discipline

Another truth Elihu touches upon is God's use of affliction for the purpose of correction and discipline. 'But if men are bound in chains, held fast by cords of affliction, he tells them what they have done—that they have sinned arrogantly. He makes them listen to correction and commands them to repent of their evil' (Job 36:8–10). God's disciplinary use of suffering is a theme we have come across before in the speech of Eliphaz back in chapter 5: 'Blessed is the man whom God corrects; so do not despise the discipline of the Almighty. For he wounds, but he also binds up; he injures, but his hands also heal' (Job 5:17–18). Elihu himself had spoken earlier of God's use of suffering for a disciplinary purpose (Job 33:19–22). Sometimes, sickness or trial is the only way God can get us to listen to him. We can be so absorbed in pursuing our own objectives, which may be wholly out of God's will, that we are deaf and blind to his warnings. And then the only thing he can do is to lay us on our backs in a hospital bed or afflict us with some upheaval in our circumstances that will pull us up short and make us listen to what he is saying. We are, if you like, a captive audience, 'bound in chains, held fast by cords of affliction' (Job 36:8). But in it all God's purpose is wholesome and beneficial, since he desires only to bring us to repentance and back into a loving relationship with himself. 'If they obey and serve him, they will spend the rest of their days in prosperity and their years in contentment' (Job 36:11).

But there are those who are obdurate in their sin and in their rejection of God and his warnings, even when it involves the fetters of affliction. Therefore they can expect only to fall under the sword of God's judgement. 'But if they do not listen, they will perish by the sword and die without knowledge. The godless in heart harbour resentment; even when he fetters them, they do not cry for help. They die in their youth, among male prostitutes of the shrines' (Job 36:12–14). When affliction and suffering come to them, instead of seeing this as the result of their own evil ways and something God is using to change their lives, they are full of anger and resentment towards God, blaming him for their predicament. It was such people our Lord had in mind when he talked about the sin that will not be forgiven: 'And so I tell you, every sin and blasphemy will be forgiven men, but the blasphemy against the Spirit will not be forgiven' (Matthew 12:31). Such a person is totally impenitent and hardened in sin and will not listen to the pleading, warning voice of the Holy Spirit. As Elihu says, 'they do not cry for help'. Such rejection of God is the ultimate blasphemy.

The principle of acceptance

Still keeping to the theme of God's disciplinary use of suffering, Elihu implores Job to accept what has happened to him as God's loving correction rather than resenting it in the way he is doing. 'But those who suffer he delivers in their suffering; he speaks to them in their affliction. He is wooing you from the jaws of distress to a spacious place free from restriction, to the comfort of your table laden with choice food. But now you are laden with the judgment due to the wicked; judgment and justice have taken hold of you' (Job 36:15–17). The expression 'He is wooing you from the jaws of distress' is the language of love and compassion. Job must

Chapter 30

see and accept that his present distress is not because God hates him but because he loves him. Elihu, of course, is under the mistaken impression that Job must have committed some hidden sin for which God is now disciplining him. But he does not major on that; his main point is that we must learn to accept divine discipline and not resent it, for then we take the sting out of it. This is the thought of the writer to the Hebrews: 'Endure hardship as discipline; God is treating you as sons ... No discipline seems pleasant at the time, but painful. Later on, however, it produces a harvest of righteousness and peace for those who have been trained by it' (Hebrews 12:7,11).

The following verses are difficult to interpret, but it seems that Elihu is again urging Job to accept the discipline imposed upon him and not to be swayed by other possible courses of action. 'Be careful that no-one entices you by riches; do not let a large bribe turn you aside. Would your wealth or even all your mighty efforts sustain you so you would not be in distress?' (Job 36:18–19). He is saying, in effect, 'Don't let anyone entice or bribe you into thinking that the loss of your great wealth and standing was too great a price to pay for your allegiance to God.' And there is a great truth in that. No price we pay by way of suffering and trial or distress can ever be too great for the salvation we have received. In the previous chapter we tried to answer the question, Does it pay to serve God? And we came up with the answer that it does pay a thousand times. We must never allow ourselves to be enticed from that point of view by the specious arguments of others.

Job is warned further, 'Do not long for the night, to drag people away from their homes. Beware of turning to evil, which you seem to prefer to affliction' (Job 36:20–21). The word 'night' is used here of the darkness of death and the grave. More than once Job had expressed the longing that he might die so as to escape from his distress—'Why is light given to those in misery, and life to the bitter of soul, to those who long for death that does not come ...?' (Job 3:20–21). But Elihu is reminding him that death will not solve anything if he is not in a right relationship with God. That is the mistake and tragedy of the many thousands every year who seek a way out of their trials and heartaches through taking their own lives. For the gospel teaches very clearly that death is not annihilation or a state of non-existence, but it leads to meeting with God. In the light of that, therefore, let Job 'Beware of turning to evil, which you seem to prefer to affliction' (Job 36:21). In short, it is false to think that we can solve the problems and distresses of this life by turning our backs on God. Affliction and suffering form a large part of human life, and it is infinitely better for us to accept them humbly in the grace and strength God gives than to tear ourselves to pieces with anger or brooding resentment. And let us not forget our Lord's warning and promise: 'In this world you will have trouble. But take heart! I have overcome the world' (John 16:33).

God's power in nature

Having considered, in some detail, God's dealings with man, Elihu now turns to the realm of nature and the visible signs of God's power. 'God is exalted in his power. Who is a teacher like him? Who has prescribed his ways for him, or said to him, "You have done wrong"? Remember to extol his work, which men have praised in song. All mankind has seen it; men gaze on it from afar. How great is God—beyond our understanding! The number of his years is past finding out' (Job 36:22–26). If, in his depressed state, Job has difficulty in finding God, then let him look at the miracles of nature and see what God is teaching us about his wisdom and power. For the clearer our understanding and appreciation of God's greatness, the greater will be our confidence that he is able to see us through our difficulties, and we shall extol his work and praise him in our songs. Elihu then launches into a magnificent poem describing God's power in the natural world.

The autumn storms

First, he paints a picture of the autumn storms:

He draws up the drops of water, which distil as rain to the streams; the clouds pour down their moisture and abundant showers fall on mankind. Who can understand how he spreads out the clouds, how he thunders from his pavilion? See how he scatters his lightning about him, bathing the depths of the sea. This is the way he governs the nations and provides food in abundance. He fills his hands with lightning and commands it to strike its mark. His thunder announces the coming storm; even the cattle make known its approach. At this my heart pounds and leaps from its place.

Chapter 30

Listen! Listen to the roar of his voice, to the rumbling that comes from his mouth. He unleashes his lightning beneath the whole heaven and sends it to the ends of the earth. After that comes the sound of his roar; he thunders with his majestic voice. When his voice resounds, he holds nothing back. God's voice thunders in marvellous ways; he does great things beyond our understanding (Job 36:27–37:5).

This is meant to teach us that behind all the providences of this life, behind the intricate workings of this wonderful universe of ours with its changing seasons and its complex structures of animal and plant life, there is this personal God who governs, guides and watches over all things. 'This is the way he governs the nations and provides food in abundance' (Job 36:31). It is to this God alone that we owe our thankfulness, our worship and praise. This, of course, refutes all other man-made philosophies such as atheism, materialism, humanism and evolution, all of which as interpretations of life on this planet reject the biblical teaching of a personal Creator and propound the theory that the universe evolved from properties or components within itself. It just happened! No one, least of all God, was responsible for bringing it into being, and we are all therefore at the mercy of mechanical impersonal forces. What a bleak picture!

The winter season

Next comes a picture of winter:

He says to the snow, 'Fall on the earth', and to the rain shower, 'Be a mighty downpour.' So that all men he has made may know his work, he stops every man from his labour. The animals take cover; they remain in their dens. The tempest comes out from its chamber, the cold from the driving winds. The breath of God produces ice, and the broad waters become frozen. He loads the clouds with moisture; he scatters his lightning through them. At his direction they swirl around over the face of the whole earth to do whatever he commands them. He brings the clouds to punish men, or to water his earth and show his love. Listen to this, Job; stop and consider God's wonders. Do you know how God controls the clouds and makes lightning flash? Do you know how the clouds hang poised, those wonders of him who is perfect in knowledge? (Job 37:6–16).

God's power is seen in the disastrous effects the snow and the ice have upon men and animals. Men have to stop their labour and the animals remain in their dens or retreat into hibernation. It is an amazing commentary on man's weakness in the face of God's power. In spite of all our technology and cleverness, when God causes the snow to fall and the ice to form we are helpless. Traffic snarls to a halt; people are confined to their homes; sports events are abandoned; air traffic is grounded; industry is affected; the life of a great city can be virtually paralysed—and men can do nothing about it! It is as if God is saying: 'Now, who is in charge?' Man proposes, but in the end God disposes.

The glories of summer

Finally, he paints a word-picture of the summer season:

You who swelter in your clothes when the land lies hushed under the south wind, can you join him in spreading out the skies, hard as a mirror of cast bronze? Tell us what we should say to him; we cannot draw up our case because of our darkness. Should he be told that I want to speak? Would any man ask to be swallowed up? Now no-one can look at the sun, bright as it is in the skies after the wind has swept them clean. Out of the north he comes in golden splendour; God comes in awesome majesty (Job 37:17–22).

The picture is of a hot, stifling day, with the sky a hard metallic blue and people so listless that little or no work is done. Again it is intended to show how man is at the mercy of God's control over the events on earth. It is ridiculous therefore for Job, or any one of us, to think we can 'draw up our case' to justify our position before such a mighty God. Elihu concludes that the only thing we can do as sinful beings is worship and revere the Creator in the greatness of his being: 'The Almighty is beyond our reach and exalted in power; in his justice and great righteousness, he does not oppress. Therefore, men revere him, for does he not have regard for all the wise in heart?' (Job 37:23–24).

Summary of the Elihu speeches

Elihu's contribution to the discussion begins in chapter 32 with his extended apology for not intervening earlier. He had held back because he was so conscious of his youth in the presence of the three friends who, being older, were therefore considered to be much wiser (Job 32:1–9). However, he quickly expresses his disappointment with their wisdom, as they had failed to refute Job's arguments. He asserts that his approach will be entirely different from theirs, for his insights are not merely the fruit of his own thinking but arise from the inspiration of the Spirit of God within him (Job 32:10–22). He then addresses Job directly and advances four unanswered speeches covering chapters 33–37.

In his first speech (Job 33) he is concerned to correct Job's perception of God as his enemy because of the suffering he has to endure. Elihu says he is wrong in this and is being dishonouring to God by interrogating him as if he were under some obligation to provide Job with the answers he is looking for. Job has forgotten that 'God is greater than man' and is not answerable to anyone (Job 33:1–12). Secondly, because Job does not receive the answers he wants, he should not complain that God is uncommunicative and unwilling to make his thoughts known to men. God does speak to men, sometimes in dreams and visions, and even through suffering such as Job is experiencing, and he does so for disciplinary purposes, for enlightenment, and for restoring people to himself when they have strayed from him (Job 33:13–33).

In his second speech (Job 34) Elihu is anxious to defend God's righteous character and the justice of his government in the face of Job's complaint that God is morally indifferent to whether men are righteous or wicked. Elihu emphasises God's law of exact retribution by which 'He repays a man for what he has done', irrespective of whether he is a prince or a pauper (Job 34:1–20). Furthermore, there is no escaping God's justice, for in his omniscience he sees and knows everything (Job 34:21–30). Finally, Elihu is concerned that Job should be reconciled to God and advises him to repent, not because of past sins, but because of his inflammatory words about God not governing the world justly (Job 34:31–37).

Elihu continues in his third speech (Job 35) to defend the justice of God's rule. But now he turns the question back on Job by asking him if he is being just and consistent in claiming that God will vindicate his innocence, whilst at the same time complaining that there is no positive gain in living a godly life (Job 35:1–3). In support of his argument Elihu points Job to the creative power of God as seen in the beauty of the heavens and wants to convince him that God is so much greater than ourselves that neither man's righteousness nor his wickedness can influence his sovereign rule. Therefore it was ridiculous for Job to imagine that his innocence could persuade God to answer his complaint (Job 35:1–8).

More than once Job had complained bitterly that God did not respond to the cries of the poor and oppressed, and that his failure to do so was itself an indication of the injustice of his rule. But Elihu's reply is twofold. First, the cries of the oppressed are not a petitionary prayer—'Where is God my Maker?'—rather, they are cries of resentment because of what is happening to them. Second, God will not answer any prayer that is made in a bitter and arrogant spirit. Job should learn this lesson and humbly wait on God; instead he 'opens his mouth with empty talk; without knowledge he multiplies words' (Job 35:9–16).

In his fourth and final speech (Job 36 and 37), in an attempt to help Job view his own suffering in a more favourable light, Elihu returns to the theme of God's disciplinary use of affliction. Although he is mighty, God does not 'despise men' in their littleness and sin, and his use of affliction is wholesome and beneficial, since his only aim is to restore them to fellowship with himself (Job 36:1–21). In his final argument Elihu seeks to focus Job's thinking upon the greatness and splendour of God in nature so as to have a clearer understanding of his wisdom and power. The visible signs of the divine greatness, in the snow and ice and in the rain and sunshine of the changing seasons, all point to a personal God who in his wisdom and power governs and watches over all things. Such a mighty God is 'beyond our reach'; therefore it is nonsense for Job to talk of arguing his case before him as if to convince him of his innocence. The only fitting response is for Job to fall down before him in worship and praise (Job 36:22–37:24).

Chapter 31

God's challenge to Job

Read Job chapters 38:1–42:6

In the last five chapters (Job 38–42) we come to the final section of the book of Job. Up to this point we have listened to the words of men as they have given their own explanations of God's dealings with Job, and we have also listened to Job himself complaining of his sufferings and blaming God for being unjust in his treatment of him. But now God himself speaks, and in a series of rhetorical questions, some sixty or more, he challenges Job to make good the claims he has made against him. After all, Job had several times said he wanted a confrontation with God: 'But I desire to speak with the Almighty and to argue my case with God' (Job 13:3); 'I will surely defend my ways to his face' (Job 13:15). Well, he was now to get his chance, and we shall see what he makes of it!

God in the storm

'Then the Lord answered Job out of the storm. He said: "Who is this that darkens my counsel with words without knowledge? Brace yourself like a man; I will question you, and you shall answer me"' (Job 38:1–3). In the previous chapter, Elihu had ended his speech with a magnificent description of a thunderstorm to illustrate the power of God. It may have been that such a storm was brewing or actually raging when he was speaking, and that the crashing thunder and flashing lightning all served to impress upon Job a sense of the majesty and presence of God speaking to his own soul. Whether he heard an actual voice we cannot say. Certainly, there were times when men did hear the voice of God speaking to them, as in the incident of Moses and the burning bush (Exodus 3), Samuel in the tabernacle (1 Samuel 3), and the voice from heaven at our Lord's baptism (Matthew 3). And there are plenty of Christians, myself among them, who would testify that God has spoken to them a positive personal word—if not audibly, they have heard it in the depths of their own soul, but it has been none the less real for that.

The truth is that God speaks to us in many ways. Certainly he has spoken his complete and final word in the person of his Son, the Lord Jesus Christ.

God's challenge to Job

The writer to the Hebrews reminds us: 'In the past God spoke to our forefathers through the prophets at many times and in various ways, but in these last days he has spoken to us by his Son' (Hebrews 1:1–2). The Bible is also the record of God speaking to us. But he speaks to us through many other avenues as well: in a storm as he did to Job, or in a book, a sermon, a conversation with another believer, or in countless other ways. The important thing is that we are so attuned to the Holy Spirit's presence that when God does speak to our souls we do not dismiss it as 'all in the mind' or even fail to hear it altogether.

A challenge given

'He said: "Who is this that darkens my counsel with words without knowledge? Brace yourself like a man; I will question you, and you shall answer me"' (Job 38:2–3). This was not at all what Job had expected. He had challenged God to come up with answers to his questions, but instead here was God challenging and questioning *him!* It was as if God were saying to him: 'Now, Job, you have spoken a lot about me, but often your words have been without knowledge of who I really am and of my ways and purposes. You have accused me of lacking justice in the way I run the world and in my handling of your affairs. In your pride and bitterness you have cross-examined me with endless questions such as, Why do I allow the innocent to suffer? Why don't I run things more efficiently and smoothly? Why do I sometimes allow the wicked to prosper and the godly people like yourself to find life so difficult? You have made me the defendant in the witness box. Well, I am going to put you in the witness box now and cross-examine you to show you how weak and ignorant you really are in comparison with my wisdom and power.'

It is a proud and foolish man who thinks he can challenge God or pick an argument with him. For you cannot argue with God and hope to win, which is what these concluding chapters are all about. It is significant that God answers none of the questions Job has raised about his sufferings but, instead, gives an account of his own sovereignty and power in creation. He wants to impress upon Job that, with his limited knowledge, he is in no position to question God's rule and government of the universe. Over the next four chapters (Job 38–41) God's challenge is framed within a series of

Chapter 31

rhetorical questions covering every aspect of creation. All four chapters need to be read in order to obtain their full impact, but here are a few examples.

First, there are questions about the origins of the universe. 'Where were you when I laid the earth's foundation? Tell me, if you understand. Who marked off its dimensions? Surely you know! Who stretched a measuring line across it? On what were its footings set, or who laid its cornerstone—while the morning stars sang together and all the angels shouted for joy?' (Job 38:4–7).

Then there are questions about oceanography and the control of the seas and the tides. 'Who shut up the sea behind doors when it burst forth from the womb, when I made the clouds its garment and wrapped it in thick darkness, when I fixed limits for it and set its doors and bars in place, when I said, "This far you may come and no farther; here is where your proud waves halt?" Have you journeyed to the springs of the sea or walked in the recesses of the deep?' (Job 38:8–11,16).

Next, meteorology and the atmospheric elements, including snow, ice, frost, wind and rain:

Have you entered the storehouses of the snow or seen the storehouses of the hail, which I reserve for times of trouble, for days of war and battle? What is the way to the place where the lightning is dispersed, or the place where the east winds are scattered over the earth? Who cuts a channel for the torrents of rain, and a path for the thunderstorm, to water a land where no man lives, a desert with no-one in it, to satisfy a desolate wasteland and make it sprout with grass? Does the rain have a father? Who fathers the drops of dew? From whose womb comes the ice? Who gives birth to the frost from the heavens when the waters become hard as stone, when the surface of the deep is frozen? (Job 38:22–30).

Then come questions about astronomy and the movement of the constellations and the planets. 'Can you bind the beautiful Pleiades? Can you loose the cords of Orion? Can you bring forth the constellations in their seasons or lead out the Bear with its cubs? Do you know the laws of the heavens? Can you set up God's dominion over the earth?' (Job 38:31–33).

Finally, zoology and a host of questions relating to the science of animal life:

Do you know when the mountain goats give birth? Do you watch when the doe bears her fawn? Do you count the months till they bear? Do you know the time they give birth? They crouch down and bring forth their young; their labour pains are ended ... Who let the wild donkey free? Who untied his ropes? I gave him the wasteland as his home, the salt flats as his habitat ... Does the hawk take flight by your wisdom and spread his wings towards the south? Does the eagle soar at your command and build his nest on high? He dwells on a cliff and stays there at night; a rocky crag is his stronghold. From there he seeks out his food; his eyes detect it from afar. His young ones feast on blood, and where the slain are, there is he (Job 39:1–3, 5–6, 26–30).

God's second challenge

At this point, with the opening of chapter 40, there is a pause in the questioning and God challenges Job afresh to answer him. But by now Job is beginning to get the message about God's greatness and power and, suitably chastened, he has nothing to say. 'The Lord said to Job: "Will the one who contends with the Almighty correct him? Let him who accuses God answer him!" Then Job answered the Lord: "I am unworthy—how can I reply to you? I put my hand over my mouth. I spoke once, but I have no answer—twice, but I will say no more"' (Job 40:1–5). By promising to be silent and say nothing further, Job is more or less admitting that all his previous complaints about God's treatment of him were empty and futile. But God has not finished with him yet, for he wants to bring Job to complete submission, and also to enlighten him still further as to his own righteous character and his government of the world. Job had repeatedly questioned God's justice, so God himself now raises the subject.

Then the Lord spoke to Job out of the storm: 'Brace yourself like a man; I will question you, and you shall answer me. Would you discredit my justice? Would you condemn me to justify yourself? Do you have an arm like God's, and can your voice thunder like his? Then adorn yourself with glory and splendour, and clothe yourself in honour and majesty. Unleash the fury of your wrath, look at every proud man and bring him low ...

Chapter 31

Then I myself will admit to you that your own right hand can save you' (Job 40:6–14).

Here is God really spelling it out for Job. He had criticised most harshly God's justice, or lack of it, in his government of the world. So God now challenges Job to take over the throne of the universe if he thinks he has the superior power and wisdom and strength to make a better job of it. To do so, Job must have the strength of God's arm and the 'glory and splendour … and majesty' that belong to God, and then he must exhibit his power by bringing down the proud and wicked. If he is able to do all this, God will admit Job's superiority and his ability to save himself. But Job, like the rest of us, is incapable of doing any of these things. Least of all can we save ourselves; we are totally dependent on God's grace and providential care, especially in the matter of our salvation. Modern man thinks he can make a superior job of running the world himself, but we have only to look around us to see the mess he has made of it. In all this God has demonstrated to Job and to mankind in general, his own incomparable justice and his superior power, wisdom and strength in his administration of the world. And thus, with Job, we are left without a leg to stand on.

Behemoth and Leviathan

In the next section, throughout the remainder of chapter 40 and through chapter 41, there follows a long series of questions based on a description of two of the mightiest animals in creation, called respectively 'behemoth' and 'leviathan'. Bible scholars disagree in their identification of these massive creatures, and some even regard them as mythical monsters symbolising the cosmic powers of evil. Personally, I do not go along with that explanation. I agree with the general opinion that the hippopotamus and the crocodile are in the writer's mind, but that we must allow for a certain amount of poetic licence in the description given. But, whether mythical monsters or actual animals, the point being made is that these massive creatures symbolise the very embodiment of power and strength, beyond the power of mankind to control, but well within the power and control of God.

Look at the behemoth, which I made along with you and which feeds on grass like an ox.

God's challenge to Job

What strength he has in his loins, what power in the muscles of his belly! His tail sways like a cedar; the sinews of his thighs are close-knit. His bones are tubes of bronze, his limbs like rods of iron. He ranks first among the works of God, yet his Maker can approach him with his sword. The hills bring him their produce, and all the wild animals play nearby. Under the lotus plant he lies, hidden among the reeds in the marsh. The lotuses conceal him in their shadow; the poplars by the stream surround him. When the river rages, he is not alarmed; he is secure, though the Jordan should surge against his mouth. Can anyone capture him by the eyes, or trap him and pierce his nose? (Job 40:15–24).

Next comes the description of leviathan:

Can you pull in leviathan with a fishhook or tie down his tongue with a rope? Can you put a cord through his nose or pierce his jaw with a hook? Will he keep begging you for mercy? Will he speak to you with gentle words? Will he make an agreement with you for you to take him as your slave for life? Can you make a pet of him like a bird or put him on a leash for your girls? … Any hope of subduing him is false; the mere sight of him is overpowering. No-one is fierce enough to rouse him. Who then is able to stand against me? Who has a claim against me that I must pay? Everything under heaven belongs to me … His snorting throws out flashes of light; his eyes are like the rays of dawn. Firebrands stream from his mouth; sparks of fire shoot out. Smoke pours from his nostrils as from a boiling pot over a fire of reeds. His breath sets coals ablaze, and flames dart from his mouth (Job 41:1–5, 9–11, 18–21).

We can easily detect in these descriptions the mixture of fact and poetic licence. He says of the hippopotamus, 'his bones are tubes of bronze, his limbs like rods of iron'; and of the crocodile, 'Firebrands stream from his mouth, sparks of fire shoot out … smoke pours from his nostrils as from a boiling pot over a fire of reeds.' But all this is quite deliberate. The message to be conveyed to Job is that if these creatures are so mighty and formidable, then how much more mighty and formidable is the Creator who brought them into being and keeps them under his control! 'Who then is able to stand against me?' And that brings us to our main question. What is the purpose behind these four chapters with their detailed description of God's government of the universe and of the natural world? The answer to that lies in the next section, in Job 42:1–6.

Chapter 31

The humbling of Job

'Then Job replied to the Lord: "I know that you can do all things; no plan of yours can be thwarted. You asked, 'Who is this that obscures my counsel without knowledge?' Surely I spoke of things I did not understand, things too wonderful for me to know. You said, 'Listen now, and I will speak; I will question you, and you shall answer me.' My ears had heard of you but now my eyes have seen you. Therefore I despise myself and repent in dust and ashes"' (Job 42:1–6).

It has been a long haul, but at last Job has arrived at the point to which God has been seeking to bring him—a humble submission to his will and a quiet acceptance that God knows best. We can be thankful that God does not put us through Job's ordeal to teach us the lesson of humility and submission, but it is something we all need to learn nevertheless. As one writer (William Still) puts it, what we have in the book of Job 'is not the conversion of a sinner, but the refining of a saint'. And that refining process can be painful, as we grapple and wrestle with God, demanding explanations from him for what is happening to us. Our rankling sense of injustice and our frustration with God tear us apart spiritually and emotionally and in the end avail us nothing. For we have to come to the place of humble submission like Job and confess, 'Surely I spoke of things I did not understand, things too wonderful for me to know.' We notice that God does not condemn Job for any sin or lack of spiritual integrity. He charges him that he, a mere sinful creature, had mistakenly and arrogantly asserted that he could come up with a better explanation for what was happening in the world and a better plan for the ordering and control of its affairs. But he was wrong on both counts and he had to learn that lesson the hard way: 'Therefore I repent in dust and ashes.'

All through history men have been slow to learn the lesson of God's omnipotence in the control of human affairs, and it has been the cause of untold suffering for mankind. To my mind, it is highly instructive that the challenge given by God to Job, to make good the claims he had made against him concerning his lack of justice and his wisdom in directing the affairs of men, is repeated in the book of Revelation. 'Then I saw in the right hand of him who sat on the throne a scroll with writing on both sides

God's challenge to Job

and sealed with seven seals. And I saw a mighty angel proclaiming in a loud voice, "Who is worthy to break the seals and open the scroll?" But no-one in heaven or on earth or under the earth could open the scroll or even look inside it. I wept and wept because no-one was found who was worthy to open the scroll or look inside' (Revelation 5:1–4).

The scroll or book is the book of human destiny. Its contents are secret and known only to Almighty God, because it is his plan and purpose for the ages. The challenge to open and explain the direction in which the universe is going, and the destiny of life on this planet, is given to everyone 'in heaven, or on earth, or under the earth', but no one is able to respond. Man in his pride and arrogance thinks he is capable of controlling the affairs of this planet and of unravelling the meaning of our human existence, but the negative response in the vision is meant to indicate man's inability and failure to do that very thing! And history reveals how true it is that man by his own wisdom and cleverness, his laws and institutions, his discovery, invention and technology, has failed abysmally to interpret life meaningfully and direct the affairs of our world for the peace and happiness of mankind. In spite of all our vaunted progress, our world is still as confused as ever about the direction life is taking; war and violence are still with us, and sin and corruption continue to dominate people's lives.

Who then can meet the challenge to explain the destiny of mankind and how it should be directed? The answer must lie, as both Job and John were to discover, with God alone. 'Then one of the elders said to me, "Do not weep! See, the Lion of the tribe of Judah, the Root of David, has triumphed. He is able to open the scroll and its seven seals"' (Revelation 5:5). It is only God himself who has the power to make it possible for the seal upon his own self-disclosure and his plan for mankind to be broken and his purpose to be made known. And he has done that in the revelation of his own Son, the Lord Jesus Christ, and in the gift of salvation through his cross and sacrifice.

Deeper insight into God's character

There were other lessons Job learned in his humble submission to God. The expression 'My ears had heard of you but now my eyes have seen you' (Job 42:5) can only mean that he had progressed, through his suffering, to a

Chapter 31

deeper insight into God's character. It is as though he were saying that his previous knowledge of God had been limited because it had been based on hearsay only. He had heard of God and learned of him through teaching received from others. This in itself was enlightening and tremendously helpful, since, as God himself said, he had taken it to heart and had sought to live by it: 'Have you considered my servant Job? There is no-one on earth like him; he is blameless and upright, a man who fears God and shuns evil' (Job 1:8). But because of the experiences he has gone through he now has a much deeper and stronger basis for his faith, and so he can say, 'but now my eyes have seen you'. In New Testament language, the 'eyes' of his 'heart' [understanding] have been opened to a clearer and deeper understanding of God's character. As Paul writes to the Ephesian Christians, 'I keep asking that the God of our Lord Jesus Christ, the glorious Father, may give you the Spirit of wisdom and revelation, so that you may know him better. I pray also that the eyes of your heart may be enlightened in order that you may know the hope to which he has called you, the riches of his glorious inheritance in the saints, and his incomparably great power for us who believe' (Ephesians 1:17–18).

One of the really exciting things about the Christian life is that we can all progress in our insights and understanding of God and his ways. Only God himself in Christ can save us, but once we have received the gift of salvation our life of discipleship begins as we make progress in holiness. The original meaning of the word 'disciple' in the New Testament is 'pupil' or 'learner', for that is the process we are engaged in: learning more of God and entering into an ever deeper relationship with him. But it is just here that Christians can be so different from each other. Some new Christians grow in their insights and understanding of the gospel at a tremendous rate. Their progress in the knowledge of God's Word and in prayer and godliness is rapid, and they have a poise and quiet sense of confidence in God which belie their short Christian experience. But there are others who hardly seem to progress at all in their spiritual insights. Their conversion experience was real enough, but they have never nurtured it in the way God intended, and so their faith remains a stunted and frail thing indeed.

Chapter 32

Epilogue

Read Job chapter 42:7–17

All the speeches have now ended, including God's word to Job, and we are now in the final prose section of the book. The epilogue serves as a fitting conclusion, and attention is given to the restoration of Job's friends, the value of intercessory prayer, the triumph over Satan and suffering, and Job's future blessing.

Job's friends

'After the Lord had said these things to Job, he said to Eliphaz the Temanite, "I am angry with you and your two friends, because you have not spoken of me what is right, as my servant Job has"' (Job 42:7). Eliphaz is mentioned by name because he was the chief spokesman, but all three friends are addressed and rebuked by God for what they had said and the manner in which they had misrepresented God in their criticism of Job. It is significant that the youngest, Elihu, is not mentioned at all, and this suggests that God was pleased with him for the way he had presented his arguments concerning the divine justice. But Eliphaz, Bildad and Zophar were not wicked or malicious men and, as we have seen, many of the things they had said were right and true. They had condemned evil and the ways of the wicked; they endeavoured to uphold God's righteous character, and they had urged Job to turn to God for forgiveness.

Why then does God rebuke them for not saying what was right about him, whilst commending Job for the things he had said? After all, Job had said some very harsh things about God and his dealings with him. He had accused God of wanting to destroy him; he criticised him for his lack of justice, and he had implied that God had got it all wrong in the way he was running the world, allowing the innocent to suffer and the wicked to get away with their wickedness! Perhaps the answer lies not so much in what was actually said, as in the difference of mindset and understanding of God's character between Job and the friends. As the NIV Study Bible puts it, 'Job spoke to God: they only spoke about God' (p. 763).

From despair to hope 207

Chapter 32

Torn apart by the conflict of his emotions and racked by pain and suffering, Job nevertheless had held fast to his conviction that God is righteous and powerful, that he himself was innocent of any grave sin, and that ultimately God in his mercy and justice would vindicate him. Even his questioning of God's justice arises out of his belief that God is true and just in all his ways. In short, even in his most argumentative frame of mind he was determined to be scrupulously honest with God, because he believed that that is what God wants of us. And he is absolutely right in that. God himself says, 'These people ... honour me with their lips, but their hearts are far from me' (Isaiah 29:13). He does not want us to use the right language about him and say the right things in our worship of him, whilst at the same time in our hearts we are full of doubts and questions about the reality of his love and mercy towards us. Let us be honest before God, if nothing else, for he knows our hearts. It was this determination to be true to his convictions and honest about his feelings for God that enabled Job to withstand the pressure of his friends and admit to some imaginary sin in order to gain God's forgiveness.

Eliphaz, Bildad and Zophar on the other hand were to be pitied. Although they were not wicked men, they nevertheless had invoked the anger of God because they had not been honest in their efforts to defend his cause. They had totally misrepresented the just and sovereign character of God. They were wrong in urging Job to placate God's anger by confessing to something of which he was not guilty. They were wrong also in stating that God in his dealings with men only allows the wicked to suffer in this life, and therefore Job must be a great sinner. Moreover, they had not reflected the compassion and mercy of God in their hardness towards Job and in the dishonest and cruel charges they had made against him. But, above all else, they were to be pitied because, although they were good and honourable men, they were the victims of their own theological system. They were trapped within a rigid orthodoxy, and this had become for them more important than truth and honesty. Their understanding of God led them to hold fast to the idea that suffering was God's punishment and the direct result of a person's sin. To sustain that position they insisted that Job was guilty of sin and was responsible for his own suffering—and this in spite of the fact that they knew him to be a righteous man. Although

Epilogue

zealous to maintain God's honour, they were doing so at the expense of truth and honesty. At the same time they were defaming God's character by making him out to be a tyrant in punishing Job, when he himself had said of him earlier, 'he is blameless and upright, a man who fears God and shuns evil' (Job 1:8).

There is surely a searching lesson here that many of us should take to heart in the confused and controversial state of things in evangelicalism today. Are we guilty of adopting a certain theological position, and thereafter defending not the truth of the gospel but the orthodoxy of our own point of view? As someone put it, 'Orthodoxy is my doxy; heterodoxy is the other man's doxy.' I remember reading an article some years ago by a convinced Calvinist in which he could not heap enough praise on Whitefield, whilst at the same time being hypercritical of Wesley and his Arminianism and even doubting whether he was a Christian! Can you imagine that? Wesley, a man of God used so mightily alongside Whitefield in the Evangelical Awakening! Yet the remarkable thing is that these two great men were so gracious and warm in their relations to each other in spite of their differing points of view. The following letter, quoted in Arnold Dallimore's *Life of Whitefield*, was written by Wesley to Whitefield relating to their doctrinal differences:

My Dear Brother,
I thank you for yours, May the 4th 1740. The case is quite plain. There are bigots both for predestination and against it. God is sending a message to those on either side. But neither will receive it, unless from one who is of their own opinion. Therefore, for a time you are suffered to be of one opinion, and I of another. But when his time is come, God will do what man cannot, namely, make us both of one mind. Then persecution will flame out, and it will be seen whether we count our lives dear unto ourselves, so that we may finish our course with joy. I am, my dearest brother,
Ever yours
John Wesley

In the ferment and agitation affecting evangelical thinking at the present time, our prayer must be that God will keep us from that rigid, unbending orthodoxy which makes us blind to the self-evident spirituality and

Chapter 32

godliness of fellow believers whose theological position is different from our own.

Praying for others

Although God was angry with the friends and had strongly rebuked them for their treatment of Job and their failure to speak the truth, he was very gracious and forgiving and gives instructions for their complete restoration to favour. '"So now take seven bulls and seven rams and go to my servant Job and sacrifice a burnt offering for yourselves. My servant Job will pray for you, and I will accept his prayer and not deal with you according to your folly. You have not spoken of me what is right, as my servant Job has." So Eliphaz the Temanite, Bildad the Shuhite and Zophar the Naamathite did what the Lord told them; and the Lord accepted Job's prayer' (Job 42:8–9).

Here is Job in the role of intercessor praying for the restoration of the friends who had treated him so badly. The sacrifice demanded is very large and costly—'seven bulls and seven rams'—and may indicate how heinous their offence was in God's sight. Furthermore, we are meant to conclude that Job had fully forgiven the friends and held no grudge towards them, else his prayer for God to forgive them would have been meaningless—'and the Lord accepted Job's prayer'. In humbly obeying the divine command and allowing Job to offer up prayers and sacrifices on their behalf, the friends too showed that their attitude had profoundly changed: 'So Eliphaz the Temanite, Bildad the Shuhite and Zophar the Naamathite did what the Lord told them.'

This whole passage, with its focus on intercessory prayer, obedience, forgiveness and propitiatory sacrifice, simply breathes the spirit of the gospel and of New Testament teaching. Intercessory prayer for others is a powerful ministry, and it is a great privilege to be able to engage in it. James urges believers to 'pray for each other so that you may be healed' (James 5:16). The 'healing' he speaks of may be either physical or spiritual. And this is where the difficulty can come in, for we must then pray for those who have harmed or wronged us—and that means a willingness to forgive. Job's prayer was accepted by God because he had already in his heart forgiven the evil his friends were guilty of. That is a perfect illustration of our Lord's injunction, 'But I tell you: Love your enemies and pray for those who

Epilogue

persecute you, that you may be sons of your Father in heaven' (Matthew 5:44–45). And we must couple with that the warning, 'For if you forgive men when they sin against you, your heavenly Father will also forgive you. But if you do not forgive men their sins, your Father will not forgive your sins' (Matthew 6:14–15).

Some interpret this as meaning that we earn God's pardon and forgiveness by our own merit and goodness in being willing to forgive others. That cannot be, since it is the clear teaching of Scripture that God's pardon and forgiveness depend solely upon his free grace bestowed through the merit of the Lord Jesus Christ. It must mean, therefore, that our willingness to forgive the other person is the proof or evidence that we ourselves have been forgiven. If, because of bitterness in our heart, we cannot forgive the one who has sinned against us, then we cannot be forgiven—not because God will not forgive us, but because we cannot receive his forgiveness. We cannot appropriate it or make it ours because of the unforgiving spirit in our own heart.

Job is teaching us by example, therefore, a very valuable lesson, but one that we find hard to learn. Peter had the same difficulty. 'Then Peter came to Jesus and asked, "Lord, how many times shall I forgive my brother when he sins against me? Up to seven times?" Jesus answered, "I tell you, not seven times, but seventy-seven times"' (Matthew 18:21–22). To drive the point home he then told the parable of the Unmerciful Servant who, although he had been forgiven an enormous debt of money by his master, refused to cancel a much lesser debt owed him by a fellow servant. As a result, the first servant was thrown into jail by his master. Our Lord ends the parable with the words, 'This is how my heavenly Father will treat each of you unless you forgive your brother from your heart' (Matthew 18:35). The difference between the two debts in the parable is staggering, and reflects the difference between our debt of sin, which God has forgiven in Christ, and the trifling sins of others against ourselves which we refuse to forgive. If we remember that, it should help us to find it easier to exercise a forgiving spirit.

Sacrifice and restoration

Job's intercessory prayer and the sacrifice of a burnt offering were indispensable elements in the restoration of both himself and the friends to God's favour. 'After Job had prayed for his friends, the Lord made him prosperous again and gave him twice as much as he had before ... The Lord blessed the latter part of Job's life more than the first ... After this, Job lived a hundred and forty years; he saw his children and their children to the fourth generation. And so he died, old and full of years' (Job 42:10,12,16).

What a wonderful picture with which to end this book! The restored fortunes of Job and the restoration of the friends, bringing them peace and forgiveness, were all of God's grace centred in the act of intercession and sacrifice. We cannot fail to see in this an equally clear picture of our restoration in Christ as our perfect and all-sufficient sacrifice. 'But now he has appeared once for all at the end of the ages to do away with sin by the sacrifice of himself' (Hebrews 9:26). And even afterwards, when we stray from God, and our Christian life becomes dry and unsatisfying, and the glow of burning love we once knew in the Lord's service disappears, there is still a way back to the place of restoration and blessing. '"Return to me," declares the Lord Almighty, "and I will return to you"' (Zechariah 1:3). There is nothing miraculous about getting out of a hole we have dug for ourselves and getting back into the mainstream of God's love. The solution lies with us, as it did for Job and his friends. The sacrifice has been offered in Christ and 'he always lives to intercede' on our behalf (Hebrews 7:25). What we must do is make the deliberate effort of mind and will to break with our present apathetic deadening condition and, through repentance, to enjoy again communion and fellowship with God.

> Thou knowest the way to bring me back,
> My fallen spirit to restore:
> O for Thy truth and mercy's sake,
> Forgive, and bid me sin no more;
> The ruins of my soul repair,
> And make my heart a house of prayer.
>
> Charles Wesley

Also from Day One

**THE RESURRECTION
THE UNOPENED GIFT**

Gerard Chrispin

128 pages A5 PB   £5.99

0 902548 91 3

The author believes that many Christians—while acknowledging the significance of the Resurrection—are failing to make full use of its great riches in their daily lives. *The unopened gift* challenges Christians to stop "sitting on the resurrection" by living in the light of the risen Christ.

Gerard Chrispin's deep concern to apply God's word in today's world is evident in this book. Its examination of the resurrection is faithful to scripture and thoroughly practical.

REFERENCE: RES

"Reading this book gave me a growing awareness that the truth of Jesus' resurrection influences all areas of our daily Christian lives"

JOHN DARGLE, GRAPEVINE

"Clearly written...a non-Christian would find this a helpful guide to a central issue of faith. For the Christian, the mind and heart are given new vistas and great encouragement"

ENGLISH CHURCHMAN

**WHY LORD?
THE BOOK OF JOB FOR TODAY**

Gary Benfold

152 pages A5 PB   £6.99

0 902548 76 X

Throughout the years, the name of Job has become synonymous with suffering and patience, yet many people find the Book of Job difficult to apply to their own lives. Gary Benfold skilfully guides us through the book's main movement and themes with brilliant summaries, teaching from elsewhere in scripture. Concrete examples, and varied illustrations drive the lessons home.

REFERENCE: WHY

"Gary Benfold has made The book of Job light reading while maintaining its deep truth"

CHRISTIAN BOOKSTORE JOURNAL